HORSE TRIALS

Eric Baird was founder-editor of the magazine *Horse and Pony* and has written widely on all aspects of horsemanship. As a working journalist he has ridden for pleasure for years and been closely involved in equestrian events.

He has written for a wide variety of magazines and has written other books including *An Illustrated Guide to Riding* (Wm. Luscombe) and *Horse Care* (MacDonald and Jane's).

TEACH YOURSELF BOOKS

HORSE TRIALS

Eric Baird

Illustrated by Heather Sherratt

TEACH YOURSELF BOOKS
Hodder and Stoughton

Published in the USA by David Mckay & Co. Inc., 750 Third Avenue, New York, NY 10017, USA

ISBN 0 340 24881 5

Filmset by Northumberland Press Ltd, Gateshead, Tyne and Wear
Printed and bound in Great Britain for Hodder and Stoughton paperbacks, a division of Hodder and Stoughton Ltd, Mill Road, Dunton Green, Sevenoaks, Kent, (Editorial Office; 47 Bedford Square, London, WC1B 3DP) by Richard Clay (The Chaucer Press) Ltd, Bungay, Suffolk

Contents

Foreword

I had my first taste of horse trials when I was taken as a child to the very first Badminton. I remember so well sitting beside what seemed at the time to be an unjumpable fence out in the country. There was just a handful of people, my parents and two sisters, the fence judge, and occasionally a few enthusiasts walking by. The sun shone, spring was in the air and to my untrained eye the horses looked magnificent as they jumped effortlessly round the course.

The following year I watched dressage as well. The grandstand consisted of just two rows of straw bales on three sides of the arena. Those who knew better arrived as the first horse went in, spread rugs on the bales and so reserved their seating for the day. There were comments from the crowd like 'this newfangled sport that the foreigners do', 'it's their sort of thing, of course, because they don't hunt', and 'it's no different from what we used to do at Weedon'.

To succeed in sport everyone needs inspiration and it was those early Badmintons which provided it for me.

Thirty years on the sport has changed. It is now much more high-powered, specialised, professional and inevitably less easy-going. There are more pressures in getting to the top and more problems staying there. But it is still essentially a very 'sporting' sport.

Whenever there is an element of danger there is mutual respect among the participants. If the judges don't like your dressage test, or at least you think they don't, it is soon forgotten when the first cross-country fence looms up.

Horse trials demand team work and the highest standards of horsemanship. When a three-day event approaches it is just that much more important that the horse is well shod and the tack is in good repair. The horse must not only be fit but well in himself, athletic, supple and yet sensible enough for the first day. The rider need not be a dressage expert or a champion steeplechase jockey, but a competent all rounder. A horseman as well as a rider, he must be someone who has a feel for his horse and can judge how much to ask of it in the latter stages of the endurance phase. Above all he is riding a horse that has been taught to trust him and he must never betray that trust.

The relationship between horse and rider is a very special and personal one and to have a good ride over a difficult course on a horse with which you have had problems previously is both thrilling and satisfying.

In this book the author has captured the thrills of the competition and given an insight into the spectator's appreciation of it. I hope that these pages will also provide inspiration to participants and a greater understanding to all who follow the sport.

Richard Meade O.B.E.
May 1980

Introduction

One of the great attractions about horse trials is the sense of involvement which infects those spectating as much as the enthusiasts taking part. The organisation is totally demanding, and to follow the sport one must keep on the move and participate and the worse the weather the more magnetic becomes the draw of the more demanding parts of the course. There is no relaxing in the depths of the grandstand and idly watching one competitor follow another; in this spectacular the crowd goes along too.

So involved and complicated is this form of equestrianism that many people seem unable to comprehend what it is all about, and those engaged in it are constantly irritated by confusion with show-jumping and the inaccuracy of accounts. This is understandable on both sides. Hence this book which, it is hoped, will contribute to better understanding and enhance the status of the sport.

The paramount consideration in horse trials is that they should be the all-round test of the equine's stamina, endurance, and overall abilities. At the highest levels, that of the three-day event, competitions are so designed as to represent the most comprehensive test of horse and rider which can be devised. As a consequence we witness not just a competition, but a marathon performance of balletic artistry in dressage, incredible skills and courage on the long cross-country trial, and finally accuracy and obedience over the course of show-jumps. It is an epic which never fails to provide drama and stir the memory for comparisons from the past.

Nor is the horse the sole performer, because the rider is also exposed to the public view and tried for skill over the whole wide spectrum of this ancient art. This, inevitably, means long periods of preparation and schooling together and involving vast experience, patience, and considerable financial expense. So the spectator is treated to the summation of all this investment and given the opportunity of sharing in the enriching experience of witnessing at close hand riding at its very best. It follows also that at most levels there is the very real satisfaction of viewing the best horses a country can produce. For reasons which will be explained, it takes an exceptionally good horse to make anything of comprehensive trials.

In my work and by inclination I have followed almost every area of equestrian activity, but can honestly declare that none has given the satisfaction, the thrills, and the experiences common to the horse trials. I look forward to each season with a sense of anticipation and eagerness, sharing many a competitor's desperate disappointment at breakdowns along the way, and knowing that with every winner there is something approaching perfection. This is an honest sport for honest horses, and there can seldom be much of a fluke about success; while for the riders I have the utmost admiration. As a horseman I appreciate their superior skills and the wonderful way in which they bring their charges out, while at every fence they meet a test of nerve and expertise for which surely only the hunting field can prepare them – and that in the stir of the chase. This is a game of guts, and as always where that is the case the sense of comradeship runs deep.

I hope readers of this book will find that it stimulates interest in horse trials, and leads to a greater all-round appreciation of what is involved. Above all, however, the tribute is to the horse and it will show that we ask some big questions to which it responds with that nobleness which is so characteristic.

There are no individual acknowledgements to be made, because the burden of this book lies on my wife and family who have attended some stirring horse trials by way of research activity. Thanks are due to all those involved in the sport who have taken time to explain their methods, to the British Horse Society for clear exposition of the rules and facilities, and to those who train and school and forever remain in the background giving freely of advice and undoubted enthusiasm.

1

The Supreme Test

By a strange paradox the holding of horse trials is one of the oldest equestrian sports, and in its present form it is also the youngest of them. It is certainly the one which is experiencing the most rapid expansion, and its popularity is due to its being seen as the equestrian version of the modern pentathlon – a comprehensive test of all-round horsemanship. The French description of this sport is a good one, it is *Concours Complet d'Equitation*, and may be loosely interpreted as the complete test of horse and rider. In Germany it is *Vielseitigkeitprufung*, or many-sided competition, which is equally descriptive.

The trials range from the simpler one-day Novice up to the major three-day international event, and at any level the objective is to ask questions which will comprehensively and fairly assess the capabilities of the combination. It is assumed that horses will be produced in top competitive form, with all the skills and knowledge possible directed to that end. So by any standards at all when one watches properly conducted horse trials it may be reckoned that they are a stiffish performance test in every sense. It is true that a sympathetic rider will sometimes take a young horse steadily for the experience, rather than go all-out for a win. Or if the going is treacherous may well ride understandingly and go for accuracy rather than speed. But always the end results will be the same:

the best combinations will be in the money. It is the fact that such trials represent the all-round test which makes them so fascinating and foolproof. The three phases are dressage, cross-country, and show-jumping. Each of them calls for thorough training, precision and boldness. To perform competently in any one phase or discipline is very satisfying and no small achievement; to excel in all three is the mark of a remarkably good horseman and assuredly one partnered by a horse worth a great deal of money, if not beyond price.

Much needless confusion and misunderstanding surrounds the sport of horse trials, although the British Horse Society's sensible decision to standardise the use of this description or nomenclature has gone a long way towards simplifying matters. Even so, terms such as 'combined training' or 'eventing' will still be encountered on occasions, and there are the additional complications of a range of other phrases and specialised terms which contribute to the complexity of these competitions. Not least, too, is the fact that riders' scores are penalised rather than awarded points, or faults being added up as in show-jumping. Explanation of the rules in the following chapter will cover such difficulties. The overriding point to bear in mind is that horse trials are organised as a complete all-round test of horse and rider.

How, you may ask, can individuals, human or equine, be expected to do well over so many areas of activity? This, of course, is where we begin our study – with a review of history, because appreciation of the background bears heavily on the answers to such questions. We might, for example, justifiably wonder when the first horse trials took place, for there is no record and we have only supposition to support the idea that they evolved gradually over time. The likelihood is that those who first used horses in combat also schooled and trained them by informal comparative trials. Xenophon, the Greek disciple of Socrates in about 400 BC, and Simon of Athens before him, left us the principles of classical riding and cavalry training, although the art was lost for some two thousand years. The military influence runs as a thread throughout all experience of horse trials and it would seem that from earliest days the emphasis has been on ensuring that army chargers were subject to such tests as would ensure they paraded well and were suitably responsive to command, and were good gallopers across country and any obstacles in their path. Fitness was a major requirement, with endurance synonymous with it. The third phase, show-jumping, may well be a modern afterthought and a further touch of sophistication, but on the other hand there would always be – and still is – merit and benefit in devising the further but not too demanding final test of accuracy and proof of soundness following the earlier strenuous work-out.

Certainly it seems that our first records of horse trials go back to the military events at the turn of this century, if not earlier. Very strong cavalry regiments throughout Europe were involved and there was a championship event in France in the year 1902 with every indication of regular competition. That this remained very much the preserve of army riders is confirmed by the participants in the first Olympic Games to include the three-day event, at Stockholm in 1912, where the host country's team took the team award from Germany, with the USA third. Individually, too, a Swedish rider, Lt Axel Nordlander took the gold medal, with German and French riders in runner-up positions. Sweden took two gold medals again at Antwerp in 1920, but in Paris 1924 and Amsterdam 1928 the honours went to Dutch riders. At Los Angeles 1932 only the host country and Netherlands teams finished, in that order, but four years later in Berlin the picture changed: Germany took the gold medals with Capt. L. Subbendorf best individual and the Polish team the silver with Great Britain in third for bronze. By the time the next Games were held, in London 1948, the cavalry was no more but still participants were army officers. Americans took the gold medal in the team section, from Sweden and Mexico – noticeably countries which had not been directly engaged in the war throughout, but France won the individual from America and Sweden.

It was after these first post-war Olympics, on the initiative of the Duke of Beaufort, vice patron of the BHS, that it was agreed to organise open horse trials with civilian and military riders competing equally. Generously, he offered facilities on his estate in the Beaufort hunt country at Badminton, Gloucestershire, for holding a three-day event and it has been held there each April ever since with only a few exceptions on account of bad weather. This was a far-sighted and imaginative move which completely altered the outlook of this branch of equestrian sport, with the result that it has increased in popularity ever since. The location was absolutely ideal, and also the patronage and keen interest of the Royal family helped to focus national attention at a time when sporting enthusiasm was being rekindled. John Shedden won the first Badminton championship for Britain, riding Golden Willow. Then followed in succession four military successes before Margaret Hough (GB) on Bambi became the first lady successful in the major contest. That was in 1954 and from that time onwards there have been almost as many brave winning rides by the ladies as by men. Nowadays the sexes are almost equally balanced in entry, with several girls riding more than one horse round the arduous courses which was a feat first performed by Lorna Sutherland, who won at Burghley in 1967.

Women were not allowed to ride in Olympic three-day events until after the games in Rome (1960), although of course they had competed regularly in dressage competition and Pat Smythe had become a legend in show-jumping four years earlier. That there was no pressure on this ruling was undoubtedly due to the fact that eventing had been considered a tough sport more suited to the strength of men, and military officers at that.

Interestingly enough, it is invariably the emergence of personalities which project a sport so that it captures public interest, and they are very much a part of the fabric of history. Horse trials became an instant success in Britain after the 1968 Mexico Olympics when an outstanding British team carried off the gold medal. It consisted of Derek Allhusen on Lochinvar, Richard Meade with Cornishman and Sgt Ben Jones on The Poacher, plus Jane Bullen on Our Nobby. It was quite something for an NCO of the King's Troop RHA to be selected and to finish fifth overall, but the success of Miss Bullen – dubbed 'The Galloping Nurse' – was almost sensational at the time. Major Allhusen was second individual to J. J. Guyon of France, and has bred some good event horses in subsequent competitions, while Richard Meade won the individual gold medal at the following Olympic Games. An interesting postscript was written in the annals of this sport when eight years later, Mrs Holderness-Roddam, the former Jane Bullen, returned to three-day event success with a win at Burghley in 1976 and repeated her 1968 victory at Badminton with a winning ride in 1978 on an American owner's horse, Warrior. It has to be said that such comebacks are rare in this sport.

We have, up to now, been concerned with the three-day event, which is the top section of horse trials competition. They require a great deal of organisation to run, the building of specialised facilities and courses, and in any year there may only be a limited number of horses and riders at this advanced level. Accordingly, in most countries there will be but a select few fixtures of this calibre. In Britain, for example, there are some five major horse trials, while seventy-three other fixtures are classified as one- or two-day events – mainly the latter. In addition, of course, any number of unofficial and hunter trials, together with Pony Club trials and championships.

While international attention is directed to the major trials, it would be fair to say that the smaller events are properly the backbone of the sport. There may, for example, be some seventy entrants (and fewer starters) for the big ones, but in Britain well in excess of 10,800 entries a year may be made overall in official trials, indicating the extent of interest in one-day events. Also an annual increase of twenty-five per cent is being catered for, even against a pattern of rising costs and other difficulties. Most horse trials are heavily over-subscribed and spectator attendance, certainly at major events, is becoming a major problem and an embarrassing success despite a general lack of publicising locations.

The three-day event is the supreme test of horse and rider, whereas lesser events may best be described as the complete test. In fact, though, they are the public training grounds where experience is gained; invaluable for bringing young horses on and getting the combination attuned for more advanced competition later on. Yet while this is true, it should not be taken as the reason for holding such trials, since it is undeniable that the majority are extremely tough and demanding, with competitors engaged to win and the horses having all the appearance of being eager as well – understandably, because they have been steadily brought on and schooled and made fit for just this test. There is the other factor, too, that those who succeed at this level must catch the selectors' eyes for further advancement, top-class training, and preparation for international and even Olympic places. Not every rider seeks this goal; very few have equines with the potential. Common to all, however, is the seeking to put up an impressive performance in horse trials to show this all-round merit and reflect the skills necessary to produce a horse in condition to complete the test.

The one-day trial still embraces the three phases of competition, beginning with dressage but often reversing the order of three-day events by going into show-jumping and concluding with the cross-country phase. Of course the questions asked and the courses set always vary according to the standard and experience of horses engaged. A two-day event is really an Intermediate one, in preparation for the ultimate three-day event. In practical terms the main difference between them is that the cross-country phase is extended to include a modified steeplechase, and endurance is further tested by adding a ride over roads and tracks.

A point which must be made is that the best preparation for horse trials at any level is in the hunting field. This is where stamina is tested, as is the courage of horse and rider in pursuing as straight a course as may be possible behind hounds, which means jumping every fence or obstacle in the way. The excitement of the chase helps to develop boldness and of course it is bred into the stock. It is this factor which helps to explain the suitability of Irish horses for the sport. They have the background, the strength, and the character for it.

Sometimes horse trials and hunter trials are bracketed together, but this is an error as the two, although related, are entirely different in concept. The former, remember, is the complete test in three phases, whereas hunter trials originated as an end-of-season competition and means of testing out likely horses over a one-and-a-half miles long course with about twenty natural fences no higher than 3 ft 6 in (1 metre) or with spread of up to 9 ft (2½ metres). Style, speed (450 yd/min or 411 metres/min) and accuracy determine the results. Such trials have been hunt fund-raisers and enjoyable social occasions, although point-to-point races are more spectacular and draw the crowds. Close on 185 of these are held annually, confined to horses hunted regularly, and date back to at least 1836 when there is record of one held in Worcestershire. The season is from February through to mid-June and whereas at one time familiar hunt country made the course from one point to another over 3 miles (5 km) distance, nowadays racecourse facilities are often used with fences up to 4 ft 3 in (1.15 metres) and some fast, exciting races run. The best horses often graduate to National Hunt racing or other branches of the sport but hunter trials are easier on potential event horses.

If these two additions to hunting experience have little connection with horse trials, there are certainly closer links with an entertaining, new activity of running cross-country team events. The first was held as recently as 1974 at Hickstead and proved so popular that the idea has spread extensively. Teams of four ride together over big natural fences with the first three to finish counting for time over the course. This is a fast and exuberant team sport and a good test of horsemanship, so horse trials riders are frequently to be found among those engaged. Still, this form of cross-country riding is very much easier than the infinitely trickier fences of even a one-day event, and no other questions are asked, so that, again, comparison is unprofitable.

With such a plethora of trials taking place in one form or another it may be thought that the horse is subjected to too many tests. Certainly the spectator has a wide choice and is probably divided in allegiance. Of course, for many of us this is the attraction of equestrian sports in that there is infinite variety and quite remarkable support for all, and surely it is interesting that the hunting field is now seen as the perfect training ground and preparation for such competitions? Hunting has many critics, but while charges of cruelty have been proven against 'Charlie' fox, the same is not true of the hunts, whose reputations are such that they would scarcely allow a quarry to linger. But what does the hunting field prove? The answer is only to be found at the end of a long run and a several miles point, running over good hunt country and flighting over every obstacle encountered. Those that can keep in touch and be in at the finish will have no doubts about their mount's staying power and stamina. Their horses will be as bold as the riders, thoroughly sound in wind and limb, and always eager to be up with the leaders. That is the measure of a potential horse trials horse, and believe me they are not all that plentiful, which explains why their prices are consistently high and why the best are internationally sought and merit such respect.

In closing this chapter on the background to horse trials, and before embarking on all the details, I think it is only right to pay tribute to the pluck and courage of those who ride in them. It can serve as warning to intending competitors – not to put them off, but rather to point to the need for full and adequate preparations so that the odds against may be reduced. Similarly, spectators will be warned a little later that enough risks exist without their adding to the difficulties through thoughtless behaviour on the course. It is, however, quite pointless to raise questions such as 'Why riders participate in such a tough sport and enjoy it' or 'Why they do not take the safest course' because manifestly the skilful horseman will always ride to win, and if there is any thought of coming down the concern would be for the horse rather than themselves.

As standards of excellence and performance ratings increase, so, unfortunately, does it become necessary for the organisers of horse trials to build still bigger courses and for judges to be yet more exacting in their standards of perfection. To this is added the pressure by competing countries for success in international events, especially at the Olympic Games, and increasingly in the background there are sponsors prepared to meet the bills for participation in this costly sport only so long as the results reflect radiantly on their commercial operations. Not least there are also the unknown factors of weather and the temperament of riders and horses, which can suddenly transform a leisurely trial into a maelstrom. From the spectator's point of view this can often produce spellbinding sport and it is often said that the paying public relish such situations although overtly protesting at the dangerous state of the going. Let us be quite honest and admit that sensations and examples of courage against adversity are essentially the stuff of horse trials. There have been some stirring events which have riveted our attention as no other sport could possibly do, and yet – and this is the saving grace – we are first and always followers of the horses, and so want more than anything to witness a tough but fair test of endurance and skills. This is what adds up to a true appreciation of horse trials.

The toughest of all competition is the World Championship, which is invariably more exacting even than the Olympic Games. At Lexington, Kentucky, USA in 1978, for example, there was a huge course enough to daunt any combination and made worse by temperatures going to 90°F (32°C). Only twenty-four horses out of almost fifty went through to the final phase, which in itself is a measure of the test inflicted. The gruelling experience, and some say psychological effects on the horses, of such contests are oft-debated topics among all concerned. They are a reminder that at the highest levels this sport can closely approach, for various sound reasons, the narrow line between what is acceptable and unacceptable by way of this supreme test of horse and rider. It may be sporting to push right up to the optimum, but there will be limits and it appears that after tremendous progress in testing performance we may now be getting very close to the limit.

Fortunately, ingenuity in course-building, progress in stock-breeding, and the timeless skills of those in charge of the horses, all mean we can be completely optimistic about the future of horse trials. I am convinced that they will develop increasingly and entertain ever-rising attendance figures into the future, especially as appreciation of the finer points grows and understanding of the rules brings added enjoyment of this all-round test.

2

Knowing the Rules

Because the aim is to produce a result from an all-round test, it follows that a good deal of organisation goes into preparations for horse trials. Meticulous planning is required for the three separate phases of competition and the end result is a mathematical equation which provides a very detailed and extremely useful marking system. It is followed by competitors and spectators alike so that the total performance, and any errors or weaknesses, become public knowledge.

So far as possible, standard conditions are provided for those competing so that no individual is unfairly treated. This means there are minimum weights to be carried, the order of starting is drawn and regulated, and time is taken into account. Inevitably, there can be stoppages due to weather conditions or accidents on course, but the whole programme is run as nearly as possible to clockwork, with a central control in touch with every part of the course and trials ground by telecommunication linkage. Those attending horse trials for the first time cannot fail to be impressed by the organisation, which indeed owes much to its military origins. The surprising feature is that, notwithstanding this rigid control, there remains a delightful informality about these events, which is undoubtedly why people enjoy them so much, and I think the reason lies in the very fact that they are methodically pre-planned so that, barring weather crises on the day, all concerned can more or less relax and concentrate on the main preoccupation of administering a fair test for competitors.

Familiarity with the Rules for official horse trials, as laid down by the British Horse Society, is obviously essential for the organisers and riders, and is desirable for spectators if they are to follow proceedings closely. It must be helpful therefore to give a detailed explanation in lucid form.

Broad outline

All horse trials consist of three separate sections, dressage, cross-country and show-jumping. The marks are cumulative. Trials are usually either *sponsored*, which means financed by and organised on behalf of the BHS; or they are *affiliated*, i.e. financed and organised by an independent individual or body and affiliated to the BHS. Either way they come under the official Rules, although of course in theory anyone can organise unofficial horse trials. This would normally have to be made quite clear to intending competitors, who would usually want to know under what conditions trials are to be conducted.

The three main types of horse trials are:

1   *One-Day:* when the three tests or sections follow one another directly.
2   *Two-Day:* Similar, but the cross-country test may be extended to include a modified steeplechase course and work over roads and tracks, as additional endurance test.
3   *Three-Day:* The ultimate form of competition, with the three tests taking place over separate days. The first day is confined to dressage, the next involves two separate phases of roads and tracks, a steeplechase, and the major cross-country phase; in other words tests of speed and endurance. Then on the final day there is the show-jumping, which is simply to demonstrate that after the severe physical test of endurance, the horse has retained the suppleness of muscle, with the necessary energy and obedience to continue responding to the rider's directions.

Organisation

Those wishing to hold official trials have to make application to the governing body, with a fee of about £50 for each trial. In the case of new events the procedure will be for the site to be inspected and plans agreed before approval. Schedules are then prepared and then programmes, which must list the timetable in detail, the entries with scoresheet similar to the large public noticeboard which is a feature of such trials, and this also gives a plan of the cross-country course with distance and optimum time. In some cases the dressage tests will be detailed.

Prizes are laid down by the organising Horse Trials Committee, on a scale which offers £125 first prize in an Advanced trial, £85 for 2nd, and £65 for 3rd place then ranging down according to the number of starters (for example there may be an 8th prize of £15 if there are over thirty starters and *pro rata*). The grades below Advanced are Open Intermediate and Intermediate and prizes there range from £60 for first prize, £50 for 2nd, and £45 for 3rd down to about £12 for 8th, where there are thirty starters. In Novice and Junior trials, which are of course the lowest grades for new-comers, there may be only £35 or £40 for first prize, £25 for 2nd, and £15 for 3rd and the 8th prize in a large entry would be down to £8 or less. It should be added that at most trials there will be special awards or additional prizes given by sponsors, notably of horse rugs and trophies. Often, too, there is a special award for cross-country performance, recognising that a notable performance in this phase is especially appreciated by the crowd. The Rules stipulate, however, that it should always be given in respect of the competitor with the lowest total of jumping and/or time penalties. The prizes described are those normally given, but for major three-day events these may be negotiated, and in the case of two-day trials the rewards go up a scale i.e. Novices' prizes are as for Intermediate and that grade receive the same as the Advanced level, with Advanced scales again negotiated – usually with sponsors involved. Where Open Intermediate trials are held, a special prize of £10 may be given to the highest placed horses not in the top grade.

This whole system of grading horses can be confusing and requires full explanation since it plays an important role in the organisation of the sport. The position is that points are awarded to winners of prize money in all official horse trials, other than Junior events. Like the prizes themselves, the points are scaled to standard of event and placings. For example in one-day trials at Novice standard the winner is given 6pts, reducing by 1pt each down to sixth place. Open Intermediate and Intermediate classes award 12pts for 1st, scaling 2pts down to sixth place, while the top-ranked Advanced class horse can gain 18pts scaling 3pts each down to sixth position. Two-day trials gain an extra point per place in the equivalent scale. In Championship trials the Novice 1st receives 15pts, 2nd 13pts, 3rd 11pts, 4th 9pts, 5th 8pts, 6th 6pts. The Advanced level earns exactly double these points.

Points awarded in a three-day horse trials would be on the following basis:

	1st	2nd	3rd	4th	5th	6th	7th	8th
Novice	8	7	6	5	4	3	2	1
Standard	16	12	10	8	6	4	2	1
First Division	24	20	16	12	10	8	6	4
Championship	40	36	28	24	20	16	14	12

(and − 2 to 12th place)

The horses are graded according to the points they have been awarded. This works as follows

Grade I Horses have gained 41pts or more at official trials,

Grade II Horses which have gained from 16 up to and including 40pts,

Grade III Horses which have been awarded a total of less than 16pts.

It is the owners who are responsible for keeping a record of the points their horses have earned, although of course a central record or check is made. Since the programme of trials, particularly in spring and autumn, can be heavy it is possible for a horse to be entered in a particular class and then it will earn promotion entitling it to compete at higher level. In such cases it may still compete in the class for which it was originally entered, but not in a Novice if it has already won three similar competitions. It could however, be allowed to compete *hors concours* (i.e. just for the ride) without participating in the prizes or earning any points or benefits. The onus is always on the owners to notify organisers of any change in status so that they can take appropriate action.

Within the various grades or levels of experience class entry is arranged as follows:

Advanced Grade I horses, or Grade I and II, as stipulated in the schedule of the event.

Open Intermediate   Open to Grade I and II horses, or all grades as stipulated in the schedule. The class is Intermediate standard.

Intermediate   Restricted to Grade II, or to Grades II and III as stipulated in the schedule.

Novice   Restricted to Grade III horses.

Junior   Classes open to horses of the appropriate grade (as above) being ridden by juniors.

The latter are defined as up to eighteen years of age. Rules stipulate that Juniors under the age of sixteen may not compete in any official horse trials other than those confined to Juniors, except with permission and then possibly being allowed to ride *hors concours*. All horse trials riders must therefore be over sixteen years on the date of competition, and be members of the ruling body or Group. Similarly all horses have to be registered, with an annual fee of at least £5 for each, renewable on each change of ownership or change of name. Entry fees for each trial range from £7 for Novice up to £8 a class.

Order of marking

Most horse trials begin with the dressage phase and competitors have a minimum interval of thirty minutes between phases – longer obviously if they have more than one horse engaged. There is a longer interval of a minimum forty minutes if jumping follows cross-country. Starting order is drawn once entries are completed, and again those with more than one entry, or a distance to travel, or other special factors, can make suitable variations at the discretion of the organisers. Once drawn up, however, the starting order is maintained through all three phases, with the possible exception of final phase jumping when the highest placed horses may finish in reverse order to build to a climax.

Horse trials, confusingly enough, are scored not on a points basis but on the deduction of penalties. Thus the faults incurred through each phase are translated to a penalty marks table through agreed formula to the nearest whole figure and the competitor with the lowest total penalty points score is the winner. Should there be a tie overall then the best cross-country score decides, which usually means that the rider with the lowest total of jumping or time penalties wins. Equal points totals beyond this are somewhat rare, but in the event then the judges would delve back to the highest tally of good marks in the dressage phase to find the winner. Incidentally, it is not possible for a competitor to be eliminated from one phase and carry on, still less to get into the prize money, because there is automatic elimination from the whole competition.

Much discussion has taken place internationally over the relative influence of the various phases on the trials, as part of the continuing process of devising and keeping a fair and complete test. The present basis makes the dressage performance slightly more influential on the result than the show-jumping phase, but considerably less than that of cross-country. Theoretically, the relative influence is often expressed as a ratio of

dressage 3: speed endurance and cross-country 12:
show-jumping 1.

So the cross-country is four times more influential on the result than dressage and twelve times more so than the final jumping. Some dissatisfaction with the influence level of dressage led to the introduction of a somewhat complicated multiplying factor, decided in advance, in the light of ground conditions and the standard of test. For Novice tests a factor of two-thirds is applied, with one-half for Elementary tests and international (FEI) tests use a two-fifths factor. All tests are marked from 0–10 and the total awarded is converted to penalties by subtracting from the maximum possible. Usually there are two or three judges and their totals are summed and divided by the number of judges to equalise them before applying the multiplying factor. That it is so involved a process is evidence of a determined attempt at fairness to all concerned, and it has been in use sufficiently long now to have proved its value, although as always there will always be those who disagree on the details.

Details of the penalties incurred in the other phases will be considered in later chapters, but the system of marking must be set out here.

Cross-country
Speed is a factor and a penalty is incurred for every three seconds over the *optimum time* set for completion of the course, up to the *time limit* which is twice the optimum time. If over the time limit the rider is eliminated. Obstacle penalties are incurred on this basis:

First refusal, run-out, or circling of horse at
  obstacle   20 penalties
Second refusal or as above, same obstacle   40 penalties
Third refusal or as above, same obstacle   Elimination
Fall of horse and/or rider at obstacle   60 penalties
Error of course which is not rectified, omitting
  an obstacle or boundary flag, retaking an
  obstacle already jumped, or jumping an obstacle in the wrong order   Elimination

The tests which precede the cross-country phase are seldom witnessed by more than a handful of spectators, and in the minds of many have little influence on the result. This is not the case, for in addition to comprising an important dimension of the whole endurance test of stamina, it is quite possible for competitors to run up penalties which are decisive in the end result. Time is of the essence over the first stage of roads and tracks, the steeplechase, followed by final roads and tracks distance. There is no benefit at all from beating the optimum time, since it is not a race. Going too slowly over all three sections could be quite costly, however, and this time factor can be difficult. Often overlooked is the fact that jumping penalties may be incurred over the ten or so steeple-chase obstacles; possibly because it seldom happens. In seventeen three-day events at Burghley, for example, the top dozen horses collected jumping penalties only twice and both were 60 penalties as a result of taking a fall.

Many people think that the show-jumping phase is of little con-sequence in horse trials, because the course is usually quite a simple one and no great skills are involved in clearing it. I use the term 'show-jumping' deliberately, distinguishing between this phase over a set of show-jumps and the jumping of obstacles over the cross-country course. Increasingly, now, there is a tendency to omit all references to show-jumping in the hope that by doing so there will be an end to confusion in the public mind about the two very distinct and separate sports. This is perhaps worth a trial, although I doubt it will work and to most people any time a horse is elevated at an obstacle constitutes show-jumping. To purists attending horse trials what matters is that the combination take the jumps with a degree of precision. It should certainly do so if this phase follows on from dressage, but in a three-day event it may be more testing after the previous day's gruelling course across country when muscles are stiff and the combination still very tired. It is in this light that the show-jumping phase adds a final and decisive test which brings the whole competition to a suitable climax with the crowds concentrated at one point for the finish.

There are some occasions when the show-jumping is so uneventful as to appear to have no influence on the results at all. At other times that factor of one in relativity seems to bear uncommonly heavily on the finish with competitors' hopes receding like frost rime in the sunshine. And of course it can easily happen, particularly after a really arduous trial and where there is a series of awkward combinations such as a treble jump. Sometimes an uncharacteristic stop (refusal) can play havoc with a quite respectable tally of penalties up to that point.

The penalties in the show-jumping are as follows:

Knocking down	5 penalties
Touching boundary or foot in water	5 penalties
1st disobedience	5 penalties
2nd disobedience	10 penalties
3rd disobedience	Elimination
Fall of horse/or rider	15 penalties
Error of course not rectified, omission of obstacle or boundary flag, retaking obstacle already jumped, or jumping obstacle in wrong order	Elimination
Time faults: For every four seconds over time allowed	1 penalty
Over time limit (twice time allowed)	Elimination

It should be pointed out that this phase is judged under the rules of the governing body for show-jumping, notwithstanding that there may be slight modification in some instances. A question which inevitably arises on this phase is whether any horse trials' riders are also otherwise engaged in campaigning as show-jumpers. The straight answer is that they are not, and this applies particularly in the more advanced events. There are bonds of interest between the two disciplines but generally speaking show-jumping is an all-the-year sport of a very specialised nature and there is little overlap. Harvey Smith, who is often an interested spectator at leading three-day events, was once chided for not taking part in them and it was suggested cautiously that it might be because the obstacles were too daunting for a show-jumper. Characteristically he responded in his own way: by going the rounds of the then quite severe Grand National course at Aintree! Interestingly enough, Captain Mark Phillips performed the same feat in 1979, but for a different reason: he thought it would be useful experience for his Badminton event horse, Her Majesty the Queen's big grey, Columbus. This talented rider is one of the very few who regularly competes in top-class horse trials and major show-jumping competitions, but it should be remarked that he rides two completely different strings of horses for the purpose.

With such a complex organisation it follows that competitors at horse trials are subject to quite rigid discipline in the best interests of a fair test and smooth order. At each official trial the ruling body is represented by a Steward whose duty it is to see that everything is run in accordance with the Rules. This official has to be there the day before the event to ensure that all arrangements for judging, timekeeping and scoring are in order and must inspect and approve the cross-country and jumping courses. This is a big responsibility, demanding of a good deal of experience, not to mention tact and diplomacy. The role is rather similar to that of Jockey Club Stewards attending at race meetings, and theirs is the ultimate responsibility for control: anyone objecting is liable to regret it.

The following Rule 27 under the heading of 'Orders' fairly sums up the BHS position on discipline:

'Riders and owners of competing horses and their servants must, under penalty of elimination, obey any order or direction given to them by any responsible official and they must, in particular, be careful not to do anything liable to upset or hinder the undisturbed progress of the competition.'

Should any complaint be made that an owner or rider may have committed a breach of the Rules, or may be guilty of any conduct detrimental to the interests of the horse trials, a summary penalty may be imposed and at the same time the matter be reported to the ruling body's specialist committee. This can result in a summons to appear, and if proven the person responsible can be barred from taking part in further official trials for a stated period.

Among aspects of discipline on which firm rulings have been given are the wearing of numbers for identification, a bar on riding

over any part of the cross-country other than in the official competition, also the dressage or jumping arenas, and such practices
as 'rapping' a horse (which means holding a jump pole and raising
it to hit the horse going over as a means of training to go higher
and clear) are severely frowned upon. Similarly doping is forbidden
under penalty of elimination and this has been subject to much
controversy as a result of widespread use of 'bute' or Phenylbuta-
zone pain-killers which can result in a horse completing a trial,
even though, under normal circumstances, it might go unsound
as a result of pain arising from a strain or other injury incurred.
The Rule states:

> 'It is forbidden, under penalty of Elimination, to administer any
> stimulant or sedative to a horse or to cause one to be administered
> in any way whatsoever with the object of influencing the horse's
> performance before or during a competition.'

The problem is that of definition and no less a personage than
HRH Prince Philip, President of the International Equestrian
Federation (FEI) has pointed out the narrow dividing line between
permissible medications and forbidden dope. Those favouring the
use of pain-killers do so on the persuasive argument that suffering
is reduced and thus cruelty avoided. My own view is to regret
the use of such substances, which I believe defeat the main
objectives of horse trials. It seems quite pointless to go to such
lengths to seek perfection in performance and then mask the
unsound horse by such means. I can remember an occasion, some
time ago, when Captain Phillips was in the lead after Phase 2 of
a major event on one of HM the Queen's horses, but it came in
crippled and was withdrawn from the competition. It must have
been extremely disappointing for the rider, and I daresay that
another owner would have resorted to the 'needle' and worked in all
sorts of ways in an attempt to get the horse past the veterinary
inspection next day, but I am sure the action taken was right and
gave us all a lesson in equestrian ethics.

On cruelty aspects the official Steward has the last word, with
power to eliminate if a horse is considered unfit through lameness,
sickness or exhaustion. The same applies to a rider who may be
severely injured or unfit as a result of a fall or any other reason.
Similarly any acts of cruelty can be penalised by Elimination. This
includes any excessive use of whip or spurs. One of the most

important powers which the Steward has is that of dealing with a severely injured horse and although in practice the decision, on humanitarian grounds, to destroy rests between the owner and the veterinary surgeon, who is always present in an official capacity, there may be occasions when the Steward may have to take the decision. It is never an easy one.

One rather peculiar ruling is that on the cross-country course any outside assistance is forbidden, under penalty of Elimination, whether the aid is sought or not. A fence judge or official may not call back or give any help to a competitor on course directions if they have gone wrong, although fortunately help can be given to a rider after a fall or by catching a horse that is loose. This Rule has sometimes in the past produced some unusual situations, in which help was perhaps offered by a spectator but had to be firmly refused by a competitor in dire straits or all hope of success would be gone. While it may seem, in such circumstances, to be a rather severe rule, it is obvious too that if it was not enforced some competitors could be given advantage through having back-up help at almost every point of the course.

It is interesting that standards of dress are laid down for competitors, although no threats or penalties are specified for disobeying the suggestions as to what is correct. Presumably the first person to enter the dressage arena informally attired would be ostracised promptly and made the subject of complaint about unsporting attitudes. I cannot, in fact, recollect any lapses in this direction, although on occasions unfavourable comment has been levelled at the tailors of certain overseas competitors.

In the following chapters we shall go through the three-day event (applicable equally to those of shorter duration) in some detail. The impression must now have been given that the organisation is strict and detailed, which is quite correct for it is a serious business testing the capabilities of horse and rider against all comers.

3

The Dressage Phase

A lot of mystique surrounds the subject of dressage, which has nothing to do with the subject of dress but everything to do with the schooling of the horse. The word comes from the French *dresser*, which means 'to prepare', and is a fair description for the training directed towards making the horse obedient and responsive, finely balanced and light on its feet, and physically supple and active. The effect is to appear in complete harmony with the rider, achieving what is known as a perfect understanding, making the complete combination.

Dressage is the perfect preparation for horse trials, particularly a three-day event, in that it is a demonstration of riding and training up to a high standard ahead of the more spectacular exercises to come. Some competitors undoubtedly regard this phase as a bit of a bore, and it is often described as the compulsory ordeal to be endured before the real sport begins. One would not contradict, but at the same time the inclusion of dressage tests serves two essential purposes:

1 It ensures that training is up to a reasonable standard, which is good for horse and rider and, most important as a part of the whole test;
2 It stimulates interest in good horsemanship, and without this feature of horse trials it might well be almost lost.

While not seen at its most advanced levels in these competitions, dressage may be regarded as within the context of classical riding and an art form. The reason why much of the phraseology is often unintelligible to the layman is because the descriptions have come down through the centuries and often there are no exact or suitable English equivalents. While Xenophon started it all, training for advanced movements became a part of the Italian Renaissance through Grisone's famed *manège* (schooling arena) movements and spread through Europe, becoming established influentially in France and elsewhere. Nowadays the homes of classical airs are the Spanish Riding School in Vienna, and the Cadre Noir at Saumur, and occasionally representatives tour abroad and captivate crowds, or more frequently former pupils with well-trained horses will demonstrate the art. Thus you see dressage is long established and represents an ideal or standard of perfection to which we can turn. It is worth bearing this in mind when watching it even in simplest Novice test forms as part of the horse trials. At the same time I would never sell our best riders short; indeed I think sometimes that they do themselves injustice by their attitude to dressage. HRH Princess Anne is an outstanding rider in this phase on her best horses, and a pleasure to watch. Richard Meade, who began an outstanding international career as a member of the British team in the 1964 Olympics and has kept his place with honour for more than fifteen years, has also maintained high standard in this section, and trained with the masters.

Devotees of horse trials often find, as I do myself, that watching a succession of dressage tests is extremely monotonous and not nearly as pleasurable as riding them. Even with some knowledge and a copy of the test movements it is difficult to concentrate sufficiently to follow every detail and fault the combination. That of course is the task of the two or three judges, situated at the far end of the 66 × 22 yd (60 × 20 metres) arena used for most horse trials dressage tests. It is marked out with letters which act as signposts or indicators to the riders. For example, they enter at the far end opposite the judges' boxes at 'A' and ride up the centre-line to the middle point (X) for the start of their test. Then they will proceed through the various movements from memory using the markers to guide their position. Letters 'E' and 'B' are on either side of centre (X) and 13 yd (12 metres) to the left of that on either side are 'S' and 'R' respectively, with 'V' and 'P'

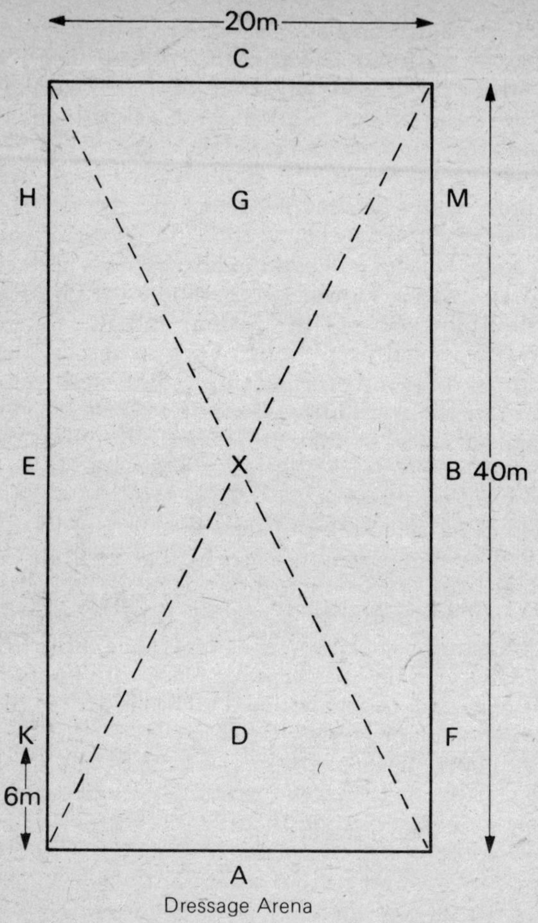

Dressage Arena

similarly placed to the right. A 13 yd (12 metres) distance separates the next sets of letters which on their opposite sides are then only 6.5 yd (6 metres) distance from the far ends of the arena. Most riders will have a similar, if smaller, arena or *manège* for practice at home, and the same principle applies the world over.

One aspect of this phase which must interest everyone is that it gives the first sight of the competitors in action: it is an opportunity for assessment in every sense. A major problem which the riders manifestly have is that they have spent weeks bringing their charges to a peak of condition for the trials, so that they are stuffed with corn and full of energy – rarin' to go in fact – so asking for strict obedience and a meticulous performance in this first phase, before an audience and in an atmosphere charged with excitement, can present special problems. The first criterion is that the horse be kept straight and going forward, which as every rider knows is the most difficult of all in such circumstances. And then there must be a cheerful and eager response to the rider's every aid or signal, with never a hint of wanting to deviate or be off the bit. It is an exacting business to be sure!

The importance of a good dressage test, relative to the competition as a whole, cannot be ignored. Reference was made earlier to the official assessment which attempts to put this phase in perspective in relation to the trial as a whole, and the multiplying factor is a positive attempt to ensure that dressage does not dominate. Even so, it is essential to get good marks, for I have yet to see a combination with indifferent dressage performance come high up in the prize list; conversely those who perform well in this phase invariably finish strongly. This is not to say that the rider with the lowest penalties going into cross-country is automatically a winner, because that does not happen so often either and is a fair indication that the formula that has been devised is quite sound. In the 1978 World Championships, for example, the horse which finished third overall carried 55.6 penalties from dressage, where the eventual winner had 61.4 and any penalised into the 80 + level tend to be unfavoured. This is especially true of a trial run in good average conditions, when the eventual winners so often maintain a good result after being in the first half dozen after dressage. The ideal performance is one which is consistent through all phases, but if this is not possible then a good start is a major help.

Each test consists of twenty movements, each of which is awarded a mark of from 0–10 good marks (not penalties) by each of the judges, and there are four collective marks covering general points. These add up to a maximum 240. Any penalties for time or course errors are deducted and the judges' total marks are averaged, as previously explained. The good marks are then taken from the 240 maximum or possible marks to give a result in penalty points, then the multiplying factor is applied. For course errors or the wrong sequence of movements the first error costs 2 marks and these double each time up to the fourth error when the competitor is eliminated.

The time allowed varies with the test, from $4\frac{1}{2}$ minutes for Novice, 5 minutes for Elementary and $7\frac{1}{2}$ minutes for the Advanced. Start is measured from the moment when the horse moves forward after the rider has saluted the judges from the centrepoint, until it comes to a standstill and the rider signifies the finish. Time faults are applied at the rate of $\frac{1}{2}$ mark for every second over the optimum time for the test.

Here is a specimen test for an FEI three-day event:

Move No.	Arena position	Test	Marks max.
1	A X	Enter at working canter Halt. Salute. Proceed working trot	10
2	C S EBE EV	Track to left Medium trot Circle to left 21 yd (20 metres) diameter Medium trot	10
3	V A L	Working trot Down centre-line Circle to left 11 yd (10 metres) diameter	10
4	LS	Half-pass (left)	10
5	C	Halt-rein back 5 steps-proceed working trot without halting	10
6	R BEB BP	Medium trot Circle to right 21 yd (20 metres) diameter Medium trot	10
7	P A L	Working trot Down centre-line Circle to right 11 yd (10 metres) diameter	10

Move No.	Arena position	Test	Marks max.
8	LR	Half-pass (right)	10
9	C	Halt – 5 secs – Proceed working trot	10
10	HXF F	Change rein at extended trot (rising) Working trot	10
11	KXM M	Change rein at extended trot Working trot	10
12	C HSXPF F	Medium walk Extended walk Medium walk	10
13	A	Working canter-circle to right 11 yd (10 metres) diameter	10
14	AC	Serpentine 3 loops, 1st and 3rd true canter, 2nd counter-canter	10
15	MXK K	Change rein at extended canter Working trot	10
16	A	Working-canter circle to left 11 yd (10 metres) diameter	10
17	AC	Serpentine 3 loops, 1st and 3rd true canter, 2nd counter-canter	10
18	HXF F	Change rein at extended canter Working trot	10
19	A L	Down centre-line Working canter to right	10
20	G	Halt-salute	10

Leave arena at walk on long rein   TOTAL 200

Collective marks:
1 Paces (freedom and regularity)   10
2 Impulsion (desire to move forward, elasticity of steps, engagement of hind quarters)   10
3 Submission (attention, obedience, lightness and freedom of movements, acceptance of bit)   10
4 Position, seat of rider, correct use of aids   10

            240

For contrast look at the Novice Standard Test A:
Time 4½ minutes.

Move No.	Arena position	Test	Marks max.
1	A X	Enter working trot Halt, salute. Proceed working trot	10
2	C B BFK	Track right Circle right 21 yd (20 metres) diameter (rising) Working trot (rising)	10
3	KXM M	Show a few lengthened strides (rising) Working trot	10
4	between M & C C C	Working canter left Circle left 21 yd (20 metres) diameter on returning to Round arena to A	10
5	A B	Working trot Circle left 21 yd (20 metres) diameter	10
6	HXF F	Show a few lengthened strides Working trot	10
7	between F & A A A	Working canter right Circle right 21 yd (20 metres) diameter on returning to Round arena to C	10
8	C M B X	Working trot Medium walk Half circle right (11 yd) 10 metres diameter to X Half circle left 11 yd (10 metres) diameter to E	10
9	K A G	Working trot Down centre-line Half-salute	10

Leave arena at walk on a long rein at A

10 General impression, obedience, calmness   10
11 Paces (freedom, regularity) and impulsion   10
12 Position and seat of rider, correct use of aids   10

TOTAL 120

The Intermediate and Elementary tests are closer to the Advanced level with sixteen movements and total of 200 marks, with a major difference being a slower and more easily controlled pace. To the uninitiated these tests may appear very formidable indeed, and yet, if analysed, the movements are simple enough, with the Half-pass in the more Advanced just approaching the characteristic high school work synonymous with dressage at expert levels. In other words there is nothing particularly fancy about the test requirements and what matters most to the jury is that each movement be carried through correctly and obediently.

Let us look now at what is involved in this action. A good guide, helpful to riders and spectators alike, is to be found in The Pony Club's Novice Horse Trials Test, and I give the details here with the ideas behind each movement as guide.

Move No.	Area position	Test	Marks max.	Comments
1	A X	Enter at working trot rising Halt, salute, proceed working trot rising	 10	Straightness of entry Balance at halt and immobility The move off
2	C MXK	Track right Working trot rising	10	Balance, correct bends, regularity and activity of trot
3	K before F	Working trot sitting Working canter left	10	Outline and correct bend Smoothness of transition
4	F between E&K	Working canter left round arena Working trot sitting or rising	10	Straightness and rhythm, bend on corners Smoothness of transition

Move No.	Area position	Test	Marks max.	Comment
5	A FXH H	Medium walk Free walk on long rein Medium walk	10	Smoothness of transitions, regularity of walk, lengthening of stride, and neck and body of horse
6	before C between C&M	Working trot sitting Working canter right	10	Transitions, correct outline and bend
7	M between E&H	Working canter right round arena Working trot, sitting or rising	10	Straightness and rhythm, bend on corners, smooth transition
8	MBF	Working trot rising	10	Straightness, regularity, activity of pace
9	F A X G	Working trot sitting Turn down centre-line Medium walk Halt, salute	10	Balance, correct bend on turn straightness and regularity The transitions Halt and immobility
10		The outline, paces	10	Roundness and suppleness of the body. Balance and activity
11		Obedience	10	Acceptance of bit, and aids
12		Position and seat of rider, correct aids	10	Voice aid prohibited

TOTAL   120

This is a helpful indication of what the judges will be seeking and how they mark, and I think makes some sense of what lies behind the dressage tests. Of course the more advanced the movements then the more discerning the expert eye. In a good test at a high level the sequence will flow freely without onlookers detecting the aids or there being the slightest pause in transitions.

How does one train towards a good performance in dressage? First you need to work at being a good rider, with a deep seat in the saddle and light responsive hands. Balance must be good and you must seek to be not so much a rider; more an extension of the horse. A good combination works as one. Since you cannot ride well without an active horse, you must work with seat and legs to create impulsion i.e. forward movement, then gradually it comes to hands which do not yield, so that instead of faster pace the horse is worked to correct its balance, bringing the hocks under and lowering the head. This is rather like revving the car accelerator pedal without yielding the clutch in that the power (impulsion) is there but not allowed to race ahead. Once you get the horse balanced between your hands and knees, so to speak, you can then work much more easily on bends or circles and other movements. It becomes a bit like a coiled spring and when gradually released the energy is bouncy and vigorous. A horse which is slack, going sluggishly, and really not being ridden, will never be creative and is dreary to watch.

Dressage may be compared, at higher levels of achievement, to art forms and equine ballet, but in fact consists of various exercises aimed at suppling the muscles, lightening the forehand, and getting balance with obedience. Especially interesting to watch in Advanced tests are the exercises on two tracks, in which the horse's hind legs follow a different track to the forelegs. Examples are the Shoulder-in in which the hind legs continue their track while the forehand is bent towards the rider's inside leg and goes forward a half step ahead of the track with forelegs crossing and advancing. In more advanced movement this becomes a Half-pass or *Renvers* and similarly can be performed in the opposite direction as *Travers*. As we saw in the FEI Test the Half-pass is ridden and it is attractive to watch as the rider moves the horse from the centre-line (L) to right or left – in this case right to R – along two distinct tracks with the legs crossing repeatedly. It is important that the head and bend should be in the direction of travel.

The jury or judges will mark each movement on the following scale:

10 marks perfection
9 outstanding
8 very good
7 good
6 fairly good
5 sufficient
4 insufficient
3 poor
2 bad
1 very bad
0 unmarkable

It is quite a good scale and quite an interesting exercise to attempt marking to the same pattern to see how observant you can become.

The FEI ruling is that by virtue of a lively impulsion and the suppleness of the joints, free from 'the paralysing effects of resistance' the horse obeys willingly and without hesitation. The explanation of that curious phrase to do with resistance is that a horse which is dodging or evading the rider's directions cannot be responding properly and going forward steadily. Moreover, it is expected to be obedient to the point of being submissive ... and still enjoy the test and show willingness.

Those who ride regularly will know about the paces:

1 *The Walk* or 'Mother pace' with four distinct hoof beats: often very difficult to ride with an even cadence, particularly with a degree of extension or big strides.

2 *The Trot* is where the horse moves on alternate diagonals and whereas most riders 'post' or rise to it, in dressage tests it is more usual to ride sitting trot, thus maintaining closest contact with the horse. For a good extended trot in the test the rider has to work hard and it will usually earn good marks.

3 *The Canter* is an awkward pace in three time count, rocking from one side to the other, and so important to get collection and control. Novice horses (and riders) tend to lose balance and be awkward, losing marks for poor rhythm.

The constant emphasis on transitions is worth noting. What the judges seek on this one is a smooth gear change, with aids or signals imperceptible to onlookers and no break in rhythm. This needs practice!

'Immobility' is another phrase which recurs, and this is to do with *the Halt* at start and finish, but it will be noted that in Advanced tests there are four halts, with up to five seconds immobility. These can be quite tricky because an active horse always wants to go on, and riders too can sometimes be impatient. A halt, however, means just that; moreover you have to ride into it, with the stop at a position of all feet standing square. A good square halt will be generously marked, with a step forward or back always well penalised. It may seem as though these are trivial points and judges must be small-minded to bother so about them, but they add up to the sum total of obedience.

Riding circles (those big serpenting loops) often sounds easy and yet is not, because so much depends on the condition of the horse. If it is well muscled up and supple it will have that necessary degree of bend, whereas if stiff it will be very difficult to get it into the turns. Basically a horse goes forward on a straight line and there is not very much flexibility about its movement, which means we are again asking for extra effort. Tests call for such movements being ridden on both reins, adding to the difficulties since a horse is invariably stiffer on one side than the other; or at any rate favours one side. As a result the schooling must watch these points. There is fault too in letting the horse dodge at the corners of the dressage arena and it is most important to ride into each corner, but yet still judge it so that the bend is right whatever the pace. Too many novices tend to let their horses skip a corner or cut it short, or alternatively make much of riding in and then cannot continue the line smoothly. It has to be remembered that the markers preceding the corner are the start of the bend and the middle marker C or A is the finishing straight and also the commencement of the next corner.

Which reminds me that a major problem some of us have is in learning the tests in order to be able to ride from memory. It is nerve-wracking trying to be perfectly sure of the movements and marker points while at the same time trying to concentrate on one's riding. As an ordinary club rider I found it rather difficult when practice was restricted and the workaday life intervened. The real solution is that tests should be practised until 'word perfect', or in other words until they come naturally and there is no problem in finding the directions but only in tuning up the horse. The other thought is that dressage work should never be done in a hurry or when temperament is, shall we say, uncertain. Better to take a hack that day, and the same applies to the horse: when it is just not in the mood and will not settle to the work then change to something else. Obviously I write in the context of training sessions and not the day of competition, but there are occasions when a horse is restless even then, or maybe a mare is in season, and instead of fighting it and making matters worse it is better to withdraw. In any case if temperament is so unusual or out of the ordinary as to put up a poor dressage test then it is invariably better to withdraw than attempt to get concentration across country – that way accidents can happen.

There is, obviously, a different problem when a horse is just so full of condition for the trials that it is difficult to control that sheer exuberance when the corn is pulling. There is only one answer to that and it is to use up some of the excess energy and get the horse settled in time for a controlled dressage test. It is not an easy problem to solve and some of the most experienced riders and trainers find it difficult. We have all seen the best dressage horses 'break' in the arena and refuse to 'listen' to their rider at some stage. It is a matter of judgement, really, working off so much exuberance but not to the point where a tired horse is asked to perform and does so in a totally disinterested way, or misbehaves because it has had enough. One thing is certain: just as it is a mistake to overjump a horse in preparation for competition, so it is to ride a dressage test repeatedly until it becomes so mechanical as to lack spontaneity and following movements may be anticipated. It is better from this point of view to concentrate on specific aspects of the work, only putting it all together on the day.

There are, of course, some exceptions and many top riders in horse trials have their own particular ideas on preparing for dressage tests. One champion maintains that her horse knows the test and this presents no problems because as soon as he enters the arena and senses the crowd he responds to the atmosphere. Another has, in the past, taken elaborate precautions to give his horse a good hack before the test to settle him, but always making sure he did not catch sight of any part of the cross-country course, because this put the animal into a fever of excitement to be off and made him unmanageable in the dressage. It is, therefore, a matter of knowing one's mount and acting accordingly, but then this has always been the way for the best results in any competition.

Most riders warm their horses up just before the test. This is something that you can watch at the trials, and personally I always find it most interesting. The aim is to settle the horse to steady pace, loosen up the muscles, and get it up to the bit and therefore responsive and balanced in readiness. Some use the lunge rein – a long rein with one end attached to the noseband and the handler taking the other and moving the horse around them on a circle. Continental riders will usually show greater tendency to rein-back and similar tests which call upon obedience. The warm-up should be timed just right, before the bell rings and the moment of truth begins.

An American competitor once told me that the awesome thing about the dressage arena is the quiet, combined with being out there alone under so many critical eyes. This notwithstanding, the great thing is to be relaxed, since otherwise one's own nerves and tenseness will communicate readily enough to the horse. By far the best attitude to take is that you've practised the test, know it off by heart, and your horse is fit and ready. So the only thing to do is ride it and enjoy the exercises, give the onlookers a show, and if the worst really does happen then damn it there's always the next trial. This is not to encourage a careless and totally uninhibited approach – of course not, just commonsense good riding is called for on these occasions.

One point which may be made is that the dressage phase can be quite prolonged, and the bigger the trials the longer the programme takes. Indeed it is usual now in the main three-day events for dressage to be spread over two days (making a four-day competition in fact) simply because of the size of entries coming forward. A good feature is that it is a timed test and so a quick calculation will give individual starting times, and the interesting thing about this phase is that other than those taking the dressage test competitors are conspicuously absent. The reason being that they have endless preparations to make for later phases and spend as much time as possible out on the course on familiarisation exercises. And this is just what we are about to do next!

4

Forgotten Phases

For the majority of horse trials enthusiasts the cross-country phase is the undoubted highlight, and they tend to forget that preceding it there are three other phases. These are important contributors to the overall test of speed and endurance, as well as the riders' skills in judging pace and nursing their horses along for what is the first part of a very taxing day's programme. The trick is to be as sparing of energy as possible; neither going so slow as to incur penalties, nor so fast as to finish ahead of time but short on reserves for later phases. It calls for careful calculation, a good deal of control over selves and horses, and also for good judgement.

Endurance is a word that is rather ill-used in an equestrian context. It has a particular reference to long-distance riding, which is looked upon as an endurance test, which it certainly can be. So far as horse trials are concerned, the endurance test is all very concentrated, being packed into an optimum time of about one-and-a-half hours only, so it is not endurance in the accepted sense of being over a long period or sustained effort. At the same time, within a comparatively short time-span, horse trials competitors have to endure a variety of tests, keep up a set pace, and in the final twelve minutes or so clear numerous difficult obstacles before the final gallop home. Endurance is a test of capacity and I think this could fairly be said to describe the second day of any three-day event, or the equivalent in a two-day trial.

The public, apart from a handful of especially interested people, do not actually see the roads and tracks and steeplechase phases, and they are hardly ever reported because they seldom make news. If taken properly they are unspectacular and routine. Nevertheless, these phases can still exert a considerable influence on the end result. This is seen obviously if there should happen to be a fall or misjudgement of time which results in penalties being incurred, and even more significantly of course if what happens out there produces a somewhat wearied or 'blown' horse for the cross-country, when a disastrous round is very likely to be ridden.

This is a typical programme pattern for the speed and endurance day:

Phase	Test	Distance	Speed	Opt. Time	Time Limit
A	Roads and tracks	5774 yd (5280 m)	238 yd/min (220 m/min)	22 min	26 min 24 sec
B	Steeplechase	3773 yd (3450 m)	755 yd/min (690 m/min)	5	10
C	Roads and tracks	10761 yd (9840 m)	236 yd/min (220 m/min)	41	49.12
	Veterinary inspection	—	—	10	—
D	Cross-country	7672 yd (7016 m)	623 yd/min 570 m/min)	12.18	31.11

The first part of the roads and tracks (Phase A) is a good deal shorter than the second and the Rules state that it should not be less than half the total chosen distance. This total will be between 10,936 yd (1 km) and 17,498 yd (1.6 km), so that the above card of 15–20 yd (14–18 metres) is about right for the big trials. The stated speed is 263 yd (240 metres) a minute or approximately 9 mph (14 km/hr) which is no more than a fairly fast trot, although fast trot and canter is more likely. This first, say, 3¼ miles (5 km) is quite an easy one, with marker posts at the kilometre stages to help keep track of time. Any temptation to gallop this one must be resisted firmly, and sometimes the pace can even drop to the walk rather than arrive early at the finish which offers no benefits.

The steeplechase follows without a halt. It is surprising to me that more interest is not taken in this Phase B, because it is very relevant to the trials as a whole. Officially it has to be a reasonable test of a horse's jumping or athletic ability, with nothing unusual about it and no tricks or gimmicks. Distances vary from 1,880 yd (1,725 metres) in two-day trials to a usual 3,773 yd (3,450 metres) in three-day events. There are, on average, three obstacles for each 1,094 yd (1,000 metres) and in practice this means nine or ten fences. They are of the type normally seen on racecourses, or at point-to-point races, when they are prescribed by the Jockey Club; although I understand that in some countries there may be very wide variation. The Rules lay down only that they be brush fences or racing type hurdles, with dimensions given as a maximum of 4 ft 7 in (1.4 metres) or just over if measured to the solid point. They look bigger but are regarded as a straightforward jump, giving little difficulty because of the groundlines.

Competitors finish Phase A and are then waved straight into the five minutes steeplechase. Usually the track is so constructed that it gives competitors two circuits of five fences, carefully marked out to avoid confusion. It is at this stage that a good speed becomes a priority, for the 2 miles (3 km) plus must be covered at the equivalent of 26 mph (42 km/hr) to avoid penalties which means an all-out gallop. This is, in fact, the first real test of stamina – the real pipe-opener – and it has been known to catch out many a potentially good horse. It will certainly fault those not adequately prepared for the pace. Carefully timed rides at home, and if possible over the local racecourse, are very helpful here. Watching the clock can be difficult at a gallop and it is tempting over the five minutes to forget it. Note, though, how the best riders frequently consult stop and wrist watches for time checks: they have it worked out in detail to ensure the first circuit is right on the optimum and if it is not the second circuit gives an ideal opportunity for correction. Finishing early is no benefit – indeed is frowned upon as simply taking more than is needed out of the horse, and the safest way is to complete the first circuit well within the optimum time because the second is likely to be slower; if not then there will be some benefit in not pushing on too fast. Should you

go over optimum time then it costs a penalty point for each com-
menced period of three seconds up to the time limit. If that is
exceeded (twice the optimum set) then it means elimination.

The second part of the roads and tracks (Phase C), which you
will remember is also the longest, commences as soon as the rider
is timed off the steeplechase course. Now the combination is setting
out on a six miles (10 km) ride at an average speed again of 262
yd/min (240 metres/min). Most will have planned carefully again,
working out timings calculated at just under the optimum 41
minutes, giving a safety margin which may well be needed. The
major difference between Phases A and C is that in the former
the distance was much shorter and the horse fresh at the start.
Now, after the steeplechase gallops, it will be heaving a bit and
in need of a breather. With no official break it is up to the rider
to give opportunity for recovery and its extent will depend on need,
which in turn will be influenced by the weather and conditions
generally. Of course the idea may suggest itself to you that the
best solution is to pull up and give a breather, trying to overtake
the clock later in the phase. This won't work, however, because
a sweating horse is prone to chills and requires treatment, so the
best plan is to go into a walk on a loose or long rein and let the
horse stretch out its neck and relax a bit. Some riders, if their
horse is really tired, will dismount and run alongside to ease the
load and save the animal; there is nothing in the Rules to say that
they should not. All the same they have to be careful, otherwise
time will be lost, which simply cannot be recovered short of galloping on – and that is disastrous preparation for the cross-country
phase! If the combination can sneak a breather at the walk and
then work up to trot and canter it will be ideal. The kilometre
marker posts can be used for timing quite accurately, and if progress
is good may even allow a further walk.

Advance groundwork pays off in horse trials and competitors
spend much more time, proportionately, in studying the routes
and courses than actually riding them: much more time. Big events
begin with a detailed briefing and then there is an inspection of
the course from vehicles driven over it. Anyone studying the time-
table who thinks that is the end of that particular phase is completely wrong; in fact it is scarcely the beginning. Those with
experience will take their time and walk every inch of each phase,
making notes and timing as they go. Then they will do it again

. . . and most likely again. They will revisit any areas which present problems, particularly the cross-country obstacles, and altogether may well walk the course up to four times until thoroughly familiar with the layout and hazards. Even then they will, if wise, update this intelligence regularly, based on information about the way the horse is riding and the problems being encountered by those on course ahead. In the case of big international competitions this information has time and again contributed greatly to winning medals.

This pre-planning comes in helpful on Phases A, B and C too, beginning to play a major role in Phase C since, for example, knowledge of the roads and tracks route will help to decide and regulate the pace. A final long uphill straight might mean more speed at an earlier stage, and so on.

It may be thought that there is undue emphasis on this time factor, but when it is translated into penalty points this can be crucial to the performance in trials. Moreover seen in another light it has to be recognised that almost any horse could jog-trot the eleven or so miles (18 km), so that as a test of endurance it has to be that pace and time are put together skilfully and these phases are so planned that almost all paces must be used in order to complete without penalty. That there is this influence may be illustrated from the analysis of a World trials championship in which twenty-two of the forty-seven competitors were penalised on the steeple-chase phase – almost all on time – and none had a mark lost on roads and tracks. It could be argued that the penalties on Phase B had little influence, but actually saving 9.6 time penalties there would have given a competitor placed seventh overall a second place and silver medal, or for that matter the competitor finishing third would have been runner-up but for 3.2 penalties through taking too long over that steeplechase. It does count!

There are no early phases for one-day trials but they are included for all classes in two-day trials, although Phase A is optional and C is obligatory. Since there is a steeplechase it would normally be advisable to complete all phases, with the first in the nature of a warm-up as it is intended. The distances covered may be shorter, as cross-country certainly is, but times are the same and there are obvious advantages in using such events as further preparation for the most advanced trials and following a similar pattern.

At the end of Phase C comes the welcome and compulsory ten minutes halt. This is primarily for veterinary inspection in which a veterinary surgeon and two judges examine each horse to decide whether it is fit to continue into the next phase with its gruelling cross-country run. If they believe it to be unsound or too exhausted then they will order its immediate withdrawal from the trials. It is known as being 'spun' and, while disappointing, there are seldom any objections raised.

This is the second examination for fitness. The first is conducted on arrival and there is another important one on the third day before the start of the final show-jumping phase. This pre-cross-country inspection is carried out in what is known as the 'Box' or 'Pocket' at the end of Phase C and this is the point at which the grooms also meet their charge and go to work, seeking to restore some semblance of condition and relax it before the re-start and veterinary decision.

The usual procedure is to prepare the horse the second it is checked off the phase and the rider is dismounted. The girths are loosened to ease breathing, a hasty sponge down begins and everything possible is done to cool the horse off. There is, of course, no time for food or drink, nor would it be sensible ahead of a strenuous course, but some give a glucose gurgle or refresh with the sponge and water. Clearly any cuts, scrapes or any hints of stiffness will be worked on, in much the same way that skilled Seconds do for boxers between rounds. All tack is checked, bandages adjusted, shoes looked at, and any alterations made to studs in the light of conditions. A string rug should be thrown over the horse's back meantime to prevent chilling and allow the perspiration out. Leave the girths loose as long as possible.

The veterinary inspection is usually quite thorough, if brief. Increasingly, attention is being paid to respiration and heartbeats, with experience built up from long distance rides which are subjected to regular inspection checks. Legs will be checked for any hint of lameness and heat and if there are doubts they will have the horse walked and trotted up. In general, of course, the veterinary inspection has a commonsense approach: to be sure the horse is sound enough to continue. As trials become more taxing and obstacles more formidable, so there is pressure on the veterinary opinions to ensure there is no undue risk taken . . . in the rider's interests as well as the horse. It used to be said that it was good tactics to trot boldly up to the finish of Phase C and so impress the committee that they would not trouble further about the inspection. That no longer applies – nor should it.

Of course the rider should not be forgotten here either. Curious is it not that there is no hint of medical inspection at the same time? It might be quite a good thing, and I can think of a few instances where riders were so keen to compete that their judgement was unsound. There is not a great risk of accidents in the early phases but there is some, besides which they can occur if there has been a bad fall with concussion in a previous event or in the stables, which would render most of us unfit to compete. There are heroines (and some heroes) in this sport, such as Janet Hodgson who in the European Championships, Kiev 1973 took a crashing fall and, with smashed mouth, remounted and went on to help win a bronze medal for Britain. That was cool judgement against the odds, but in other circumstances retirement is no disgrace, and has some merit.

The rider uses this break, then, to freshen up, absorb any news about the cross-country going, and probably flop into a seat to relax the muscles. Let the assistants take care of the horse, these precious minutes are for recovery and mental preparation for the test ahead. It is important to be in the right frame of mind at this stage, although inevitably the pressure is building up all the time. This is particularly true of those who, having tried their horses over the endurance phases, sense that they are not in quite the condition they should be: in short they have taken some nursing through and probably scraped through the inspection as well. Clearly the thought of such a mount over the most difficult section of the trial is daunting. The wonder is that nearly all go on.

The answer is that at this stage in the Box, counting down to the start of the cross-country there is little that can be done. The rider is part-way through and there is no going back if the horse is sound (and they usually are at this point) so the mood has to be one of determination. It helps, obviously, if the reports given are not all gloom and dismay over the state of the course and the toll it is taking, but factual briefing is a help and has to be taken. Besides the odds are then shortening.

One rider of great ability once stated that at this point in trials she went to the loo and then prayed. If you think about it you may smile and consider, as I do, that that is a dashed sight more positive than hanging about being nervous and probably upsetting the horse.

Ten minutes passes very rapidly in such circumstances, so now it is time for the final check-over, doing the girth up well, and getting right back to instant readiness to tackle the next phase. We shall now have to look at the course and see what is involved, before considering how it will be ridden.

5

The Cross-country Course

To most people the cross-country course at a major horse trials is quite formidable, with its variety of seemingly huge obstacles built of solid timber, and with walls, dykes and water all contributing hazards. Each successive year the names of these obstacles sound in the ears, bringing memories of former epic occasions and sometimes near tragedy, so that they come to have a haunting ring about them but one calculated to stir the blood of enthusiasts wherever they meet. I know one good rider, now retired, who swears that his stomach goes into a knot at the very sight of Badminton's famous Luckington Lane crossing, and so it is for all who follow the events. What, though, is the aim of this particular phase?

The best definition I have heard was that by Sheila Willcox, herself a most outstanding former trials competitor, who described this phase as thoroughly testing the 'courage, skill and judgement' of both horse and rider. And yet it is even more than that with preparation playing a significant part, and also determination and the will to progress through from green Novice right up to the highest levels of Advanced competition. Most commentators describe the cross-country as the 'centre-piece' of horse trials, which rather suggests that the course is there merely for decorative purposes, and it is more correct to think of it as the focal point of interest. The course certainly has a magnetic appeal for spectators, notwithstanding the constant threat of hearing the sickening thud of flesh on solid obstacle – or possibly because of it. It does take courage to ride at such fences – they must never be called 'jumps' incidentally – and a good many competitors understandably display nervous signs even while on course – often to the amusement of onlookers.

So there is no doubt that at any level of competition the cross-country course can be depended upon to stretch horse and rider to full extent, and fulfil its role within the wider context of the trial.

Do always remember that point: cross-country is only a part of the whole, even if a rather dramatic and exciting part compared to the rest. So how do those responsible go about asking the questions necessary to ensure a formidable test?

To start with it has to be recognised that course-building calls for a high degree of skill and ingenuity, it is also a very responsible task, and to my mind rather a thankless one too. If a course rides too well and the majority of competitors escape penalties, then it will not have operated as it should have done. Spectators will have had a dull day of it, and everyone will be pondering whether standards aren't getting too soft, and course-designers too old. But should the course be so big as to cause even one accident then feelings veer round at once, and the designers are accused of being blood-thirsty and much too demanding.

Even when a course is quite 'tame' and ordinary the weather can add a multiplying factor which turns it into a major hazard. This applies obviously to rain and wind, but also to extreme heat which exacts a deadly toll on the energies of horses and riders so that they are flagging even before they get to the cross-country phase, which then assumes nightmarish proportions when it might otherwise be quite an ordinary trial.

One of our outstanding horse trials personalities with most skill in course construction is Lt. Colonel F. W. C. Weldon, who is director of the Badminton horse trials and was a member of Britain's gold medal winning team in the 1956 Olympic Games as well as individual bronze medallist. He has been quoted often as saying that it is quite all right to frighten the riders, but what course-builders must not do is harm the horses. It is rather a neat summary, even if in print one cannot convey the image of the impish grin which is the accompaniment.

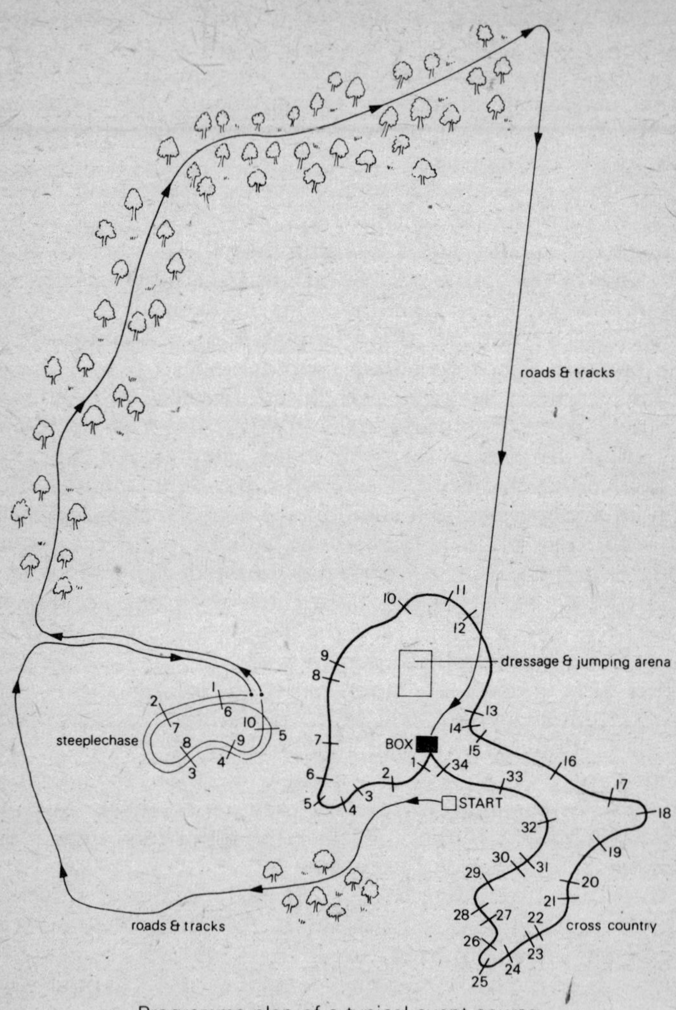

Programme plan of a typical event course

Officially the Advanced, Open Intermediate and Intermediate one-day courses are laid down as being not less than 2 miles, and not more than 2½ miles (3–3½ km) long, and having eight to twelve obstacles to the mile. The Novice cross-country course will be not less than a mile and not more than a mile and three-quarters (1.6–2.8 km) long, with a total of sixteen or twenty obstacles. This means on average there is about five and a half minutes in which to complete at the optimum time of 656 yd/min (600 metres/min). For Novices the speed is down to 575 yd/min (525 metres/min), giving them an extra minute or so. With the two-day event the course goes up to about 4 miles (6 km) at a speed of 624 yd/min (570 metres/min) with the same ratio of obstacles. Then, of course, in the major three-day events the distance rises to between 4,921 yd (4,500 metres) and 8,104 yd (7,410 metres) which is over 4½ miles (7 km); an Olympics course can go to 5 miles (8 km). Much depends on what is at stake and this bears on the total decisions about the nature of the course. For example if an important international event is in the offing then even the normal home three-day event fixtures tend to have much bigger courses by way of preparation and to assist in the selection of national team representatives. Conversely, if it is known that there are no squad requirements at the time, and possibly a need to encourage the youngsters, a somewhat easier task may be set. It is recognised that over-facing novice horses can discourage and spoil a good prospect for the future.

A 4 mile (6 km) or so course at time of 624 yd/min (570 metres/min) means a rating of 21½ mph (35 km/hr), leaving little time to hang about in order to avoid penalties. In fact the course has to be ridden at a gallop the whole way, unless for any reason a combination has motored on faultlessly and has time in hand when the pace may just drop back on a tricky section or to save the animal that is getting blown rapidly.

Now what makes a typical three-day event course? In an ordinary sort of competition the phase extends some 3½ miles (5–6 km). There are between thirty-two and thirty-four obstacles and Rules state that they must all be 'solid, fixed and imposing' and as far as possible be in their natural state. Each obstacle must, as far as possible, present the same problem throughout the competition: in other words it must not vary between times. All are numbered and flagged to indicate either end of the jump area, and the course as such is roped off in an endeavour to keep the galloping area

Cross-country Obstacles

Lamb Creep

Elephant Trap

Watertrough

Woodpile

Pardubice Taxis

Dog Kennels

The Whitbread Bar

Arrowhead

clear of spectators. From the 'Off' the first two or so obstacles will tend to be relatively easy, recognising that the horse must get into its stride and be settled to a steady rhythm after the ten minutes rest period. The rider too must get into the swing, so it is as well that no special problems be presented straight away. Designers always say they like the first especially to look like a typical cross-country obstacle, and usually it is a solid log, log over a wall or wagon, or maybe a double row of barrels if there is a sponsor's interests properly at stake. On then to another typical warming-up obstacle at about the same height of say 3 ft 9 in (1.07 metres) against the maximum of 3 ft 11 in (1.19 metres) which will not, probably, appear very big for an Advanced class. Brush fences measure from the solid part and so may go a bit higher. Where there is both height and spread, such as at an oxer or an open ditch, then the highest point is limited to 5 ft 11 in (1.8 metres) and the base to 9 ft 2 in (2.79 metres). As a guide this goes down to 4 ft (1.2 metres) height for Novices.

So with these restrictions imposed the real interest lies not so much in measurements, although these count for much, but in the wide variety of designs and sheer solidity of the materials they are fashioned from to such good effect. At about No. 3 on course we start getting a more typical sample of the sort of obstacles the course has to offer. In nearly every case the designers put something rather special in here; one which will ask a question of both horse and rider. Usually after that they do not come much bigger, but in greater variety, with all manner of devices being used to produce a suitable test of courage and endurance, and with it a fair amount of entertainment even if this is never admitted to be one of the objectives.

There are some obstacles which appear constant features of the horse trials scene, so much so that they are worth more detailed explanation, otherwise they will remain mere names until eventually seen on course. One of these is the Coffin, originally a post and rails fence followed by a ditch and then a further post and rails out. So far as I know it was not so-called for any sepulchral reasons, but possibly from the shape of the ditch and its sunken appearance between the outer fences. It made a most effective cross-country obstacle and appears continuously in later versions. There was one in the last World Championships which produced three refusals and an elimination. It, too, was two post and rail sets, but with low cunning the designers had placed them on different levels so that there was a big jump out. They counted then as two obstacles but this does not always seem to be the case. The famous Ledyard (USA) trials has its Coffin and this one is infamous for catching combinations out. In appearance it is a big oval with two rails all round and a ditch in the centre with rails across. So again it means jumping in, then two or so strides and across the 'coffin' two strides and out again – quite a tricky one. Another version has what are called stockade fences instead of rails. These are upright, solid-looking posts close together, and the outwards section is higher up a hill and so appears even more formidable, although in fact most horses seem undaunted by it.

There are variations on posts and rails, of course, since these are the most readily available and apt natural materials for constructing obstacles. Some are trickily placed, especially into woodland or spinney, and with more than one choice open to the combination as to the direction in which they jump. The reason behind this is that the easy way is often the longest or has the most difficult turn. Conversely, the highest rails or trappy position can offer a quick turn and save minutes on course.

A 'Trakehner' is a formidable looking rail invariably up to 3 ft 10 in (1.1 metres) and with the 'rail' a hefty log set over a 9 ft 2 in (2.7 metres) spread ditch. It is daunting to onlookers, yet horses seem to think it is straightforward and jump readily. There have been instances of hind legs rapping the log. Another way builders have with timber is to set post and rails into a variety of shapes – zig-zags over a ditch, or double rails to be cleared as one with a 6 ft (1.8 metres) or so spread between them. Bad enough as it is, and more so when placed at an angle, uphill or made awkward. Personally, I always think that rails which are sloped are doubly tricky – remember they can involve a spread of about 8 ft (2.4 metres), One such, designed by Frank Weldon, is Badminton's 'Elephant trap', and well named it is too. His comment on it bears repeating: 'Riders always treat this with respect, which is a typical example of the psychological effect of a hole in the ground. No one would think twice about such a triple bar on level ground and any horse which clears the top rail is bound to land well beyond the ditch, but still the nagging doubt understandably remains.' Well I must own that it does not seem to catch any who take it boldly and straight, but stand close up to those massive timbers sloping over the ditch and you can have nightmares about horse and rider falling through it. In part, perhaps, this is due to memories of a very big four-sided obstacle at Kiev in 1973 which trapped several horses and caused much pain. The point being that a big one which is set right presents few problems, and it is those which deceive in some way of which riders must be wary.

Stone walls usually feature regularly and rightly as part of the cross-country scenery, and even though up to maximum height they are not difficult. Here again, however, there is often an option to jump across the corners of adjoining walls or gate, thus saving valuable seconds, whereas the straight and easy way over can mean a difficult incline or turn.

Water is invariably a feature of most cross-country courses, ideally so when there is a natural lake or stream which can be made an integral part of the test. It is obviously important that a horse should take water as an obstacle; besides it makes absolutely first-class drama for spectators and usually the worst the riders receive is a ducking. To their credit I have never seen any take it in an unsporting way – best of all has been Captain Mark Phillips with many photographs to his credit showing him with legs up in the air draining the water from his riding boots. A jolly sensible thing to do incidentally. Badminton's lake comes at a convenient halfway stage and forms three obstacles taking a rail in and another out, with variations adding a boat-house or upturned dinghy and bank with various options open. Burghley, its counterpart, has a 'Trout Hatchery' coming as No. 26 and farther round the course and is more difficult, being a narrow end of the lake with steep banking in and out and altogether more confined. Problems come at water through inexperience and not everyone can give their horses regular schooling in this situation, although open water jumps are common enough. The trick is to ride cautiously in, even under the pressure of the clock, for the big splash and pressure of the water can be disturbing and upset the horse's pace more than a bit.

From being down into the water the other extreme is being up in the air, or rather climbing ramps and banks and jumping off at the top. These are spectacular, rather than particularly difficult additions to the course although in the World Championships building a Normandy Bank for the jump into the Lake was rather much. In some cases use is made of a quarry or ground feature in order to add interest to the course, and frequently there are alternatives leading to the bank with the most difficult and tortuous approach often the quickest and the deceptively easy ramp not what it seems.

Then of course a special feature of cross-country is the rather gimmicky but still serious type of obstacles, often adaptations from designs produced for major international trials. One example which has stayed with us is known as the 'Pardubice taxis', a name taken from a notoriously difficult steeplechase course in Czechoslovakia from which this obstacle was adapted. The Lexington dog kennels are railed enclosures with mock kennels within to distract. They count as two obstacles, but, in fact, involve three jumps. Their name takes us back some years to a previous event. Water-troughs, bridges, brewers' drays, hay-racks, pavilions, and the like are all grist to the course designers plans and they turn them into interesting obstacles which are, sometimes surprisingly, jumped without signs of doubts by well-trained horses.

The final obstacle is often the most intriguing since it is often built as a gesture to the sponsors of the trials, and acts as a most effective advertisement into the bargain. I can think of two famous ones in particular in this respect: The Whitbread bar at Badminton, 3 ft 10 in (1.1 metres) complete with roof, bar counter to jump, and windows on either side. How a horse can jump into and through such a front I cannot imagine, except that it has the benefit of a sight of home through it. Then Burghley has its 'Raleigh Chopper', appropriately named after a certain type of bicycle often seen ridden by stewards around this course. In fact this one consists of a guillotine with blade suspended overhead and a dip in the centre of the platform which is human head-shaped. It's good to finish such a course with a wry sense of humour isn't it?

In passing it should be said that there used to be a further Phase E on the finishing straight, known as the 'Run-in', over two-thirds of a mile (1 km). This is no longer the case and after clearing the final obstacle the rider simply gallops the horse in towards the finishing line, endeavouring to catch up a valuable final second or so before the timing checks off.

Now so far we have been discussing the cross-country phase in Advanced terms and it should be stated that the principle is the same at any level, except that severity of the test is clearly reduced. It must be pitched according to the standard of the competitors, by which we tend to mean horses rather than riders (although sometimes I wonder about this). It is worth adding that the Pony Club is an invaluable training ground for young riders and their trials are over about 1 mile (1.6 km) and rather longer for championships. They run to 3 ft 6 in (1 metre) high obstacles with spreads up to about 7 ft (2 metres). They are against the clock at 437 yd/min (400 metres/min). The fact that the pattern is similar in most respects to adult trials means that they are ideal preparation for the future. Overall there is ample scope in horse trials for all levels and even the Novice Riding Club events, run for amusement and experience, can be very entertaining to either ride in or watch from the side of the course.

The system of penalising horses was explained in an earlier chapter but the definition of a fault on cross-country needs perhaps further examination. It is useful to have the detail whether following on course or watching from home on television. Sometimes where a situation is not clear-cut considerable and even heated discussion can arise. The answers are contained in the following official definition of fault:

A horse is considered to have *refused* if it stops in front of the obstacle to be jumped. Stopping, provided it is followed immediately by a standing jump, is not penalised. If the halt is sustained or if the horse steps back even a single pace, voluntarily or not, this constitutes a refusal. If a horse that has already stepped back once, even a single pace, is then re-presented at the obstacle and halts or steps back a second time, this constitutes a second refusal, and so on. (20 penalties 1st time, 40 second time, 3rd Elimination.)

A horse is considered to have *run out* if it avoids an obstacle to be jumped and runs out to one side or the other.

A horse is considered to have circled if it crosses its original track, from whichever direction, while negotiating or attempting to negotiate an obstacle. If a horse completes a circle while being re-presented at the obstacle after a refusal or a run-out, it is only penalised for the refusal or run-out. (Penalty for circle or run-out same as refusal.)

A rider is considered to have *fallen* when separated from the horse, which has not fallen, in such a way as to necessitate re-mounting or vaulting into the saddle. (A fall equals 60 penalties.)

A horse is considered to have fallen when the shoulder and

Richard Meade OBE

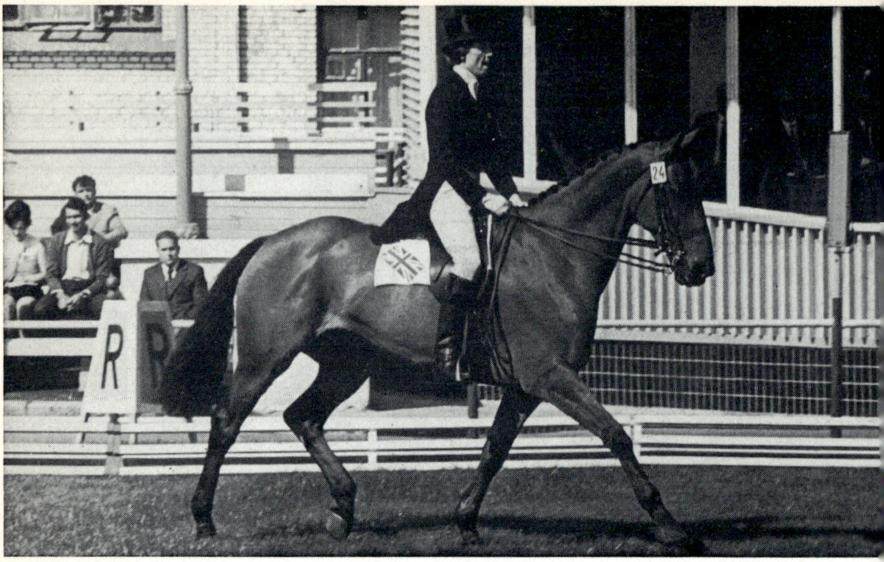

Marjorie Comerford (GB) on The Ghillie in the dressage phase. The top hat
and tail coat are traditional.

Here's a good-looking trials horse, Good Mixture, ridden by Mike Plumb of
the USA. It's got class, good action and balance.

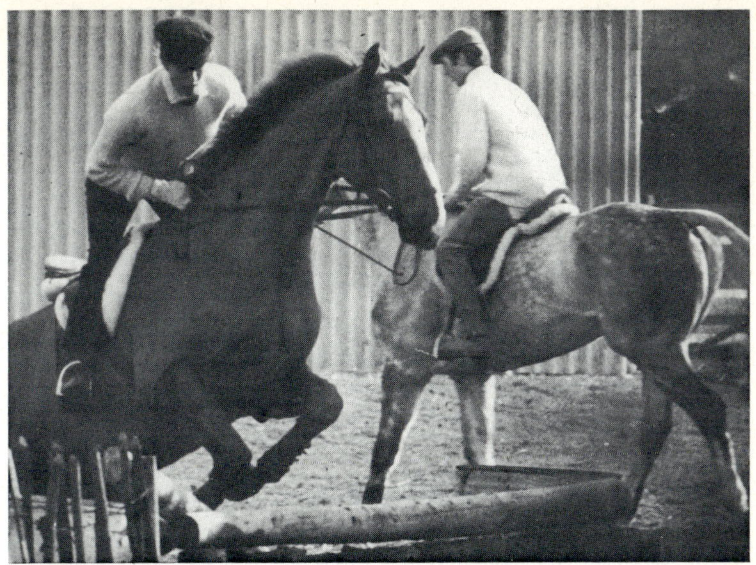

How champions are made – Princess Anne and her husband working their horses in the practice arena. It is a daily task in preparation for a big trial and essential in order to get them fit.

Tack – Niccolo Recchi of Italy on Smoke Ring in the Junior European Championships. A typical turnout for trials – note the rider's wrist watch, safety helmet with silks over. The horse's bridle has a crossed noseband, simple snaffle bit with stoppers to stop it sliding. The saddle is doubly secure with breastplate and neck strap and the horse's legs are well protected with brushing boots.

The horse that shook the sport. Lorna Sutherland (now Mrs Clarke) won Badminton in 1968 on the skewbald Popadom, whose dam pulled a cart. Looking on are HM The Queen, Queen Mother, the Duke of Beaufort and other members of the house party at Badminton.

Here's a fine action shot – the moment when Princess Anne clinched the European Championship title in 1971. Doublet was in difficulties at the water and it shows. Skilled riding aided recovery and they went on to win against the pick of competitors from nine countries.

Horse straddled – one of the worst cross country obstacles ever. This was at Kiev in 1973. There were twenty fallers here and some heroic riding. On the rails is Iller and the rider, Gorna Benetsson of Sweden, is in the ditch below.

G. Breisner from Sweden with Ultimus getting out of difficulties after a fall at the water.

Lively action fall – Tomi Gretener of Switzerland parts company with Camas Park.

The Show-jumping phase – this is a memorable American team, winners of the World Championships at Burghley in 1974, marking that country's return to the top in this sport. Left to right: Mike Plumb, Denny Emmerson, Don Sachey and Bruce Davidson.

Hazel Booth of GB in action on cross-country. The horse has a martingale fitted to check head carriage.

quarters have touched either the ground or the obstacle and the ground. (Penalty same as for rider fall.)

How does a rider approach the cross-country phase? This is an all-important question, and clearly there will be different answers in almost every case. In principle competitors will have certain guidelines in mind and these are what we should consider next to gain a better insight, whether as spectators or ambitious future competitors at any level. We remember first that this is the most daunting phase and so preparation has been thorough. The next step is to get to know the course and individual obstacles on it. Now while we have previously discussed aspects of this, it would be best to look at it here through the rider's eyes to see what impression the whole thing makes. To us a course walk may be to find the most likely spot for thrills and spills but to the competitor it represents the making of a blueprint which can make the difference between success and failure.

For those taking part a briefing is the first item on the programme and it is a Rule that the cross-country course must be open for inspection by competitors as early as possible on the day before the event, and a plan put on display which details course and length with time details, the number of obstacles and any compulsory turning points. There may be a tour of the course then in groups, but this will really only give the overall impression. The next inspection is an individual one, or perhaps with the trainer and maybe the horse owner. This is when the brain-work begins and tactics are worked out.

What would you assess first of all? Not the size of the biggest obstacle, I think, but rather the state of the ground, or 'going' as it is called. This, you see, can have a major influence on speed and tactics, and should it be very heavy, holding ground with a tendency to be wet, then it will take more energy to ride it and a careful eye on the stop-watch throughout will be needed. Then again such conditions will tend to determine the best approach to various obstacles. If drawn late in the starting lists, and with a shower of rain having fallen recently, then the ground is going to be pretty 'poached' or churned up in awkward places and it could be that emphasis on safety will require thought. Or again, of course, it may well be that the ground is rock hard and conditions hot, and that would call for assessment because other routes approaching the obstacles could be open and there may be ways of saving the horse from hard and jarring going. Even the effects of sunlight and shade on the obstacles or track, particularly through woodland, need thought and the more so if one's horse is inclined to 'spook' or jump at shadows.

Next we have time in mind – and by the way one is not allowed to drive around the course stop-watch in hand. You can and should pace it all out, establishing the shortest routes, bearing in mind that these are not necessarily the right ones for you. It is more a case of taking a decision on the right approach in the circumstances of the day to each obstacle. Suit this to time factors, your horse's capabilities, and with an eye to a safe and clear round of the course. It is always helpful to know distances, in terms of horse strides rather than feet or metres. This is particularly applicable to combinations where it may be easy enough to take the first part, but then if unprepared the horse will not be gathered up in time for the second, so pacing out the number of strides can be valuable information. Recognising such problems helps also to ensure that the rider is properly prepared personally, well-balanced and confident.

Another factor is knowing when the going will be tough and asking for impulsion in the right place. A long ramp, for example, may bring a sluggish combination to a near halt but if going strongly enough the horse will be atop it and ready for the jump off without being aware of the fact. The same is true at the water, remembering that while a horse going well is more likely to go on and get its feet wet, if it plunges in too fast a stop is a possibility. No doubt most people have seen photographs of trial riders wading about in water jumps, perhaps even thinking it rather silly and unnecessary. Not so, because they need to know the depth of water and the state of the bottoming and whether there are any hidden hazards there. Equally it will be obvious that a depth of holding soggy clay would have a different effect on a horse than a shallow gravel bed.

When it comes to those massive logs and tricky obstacles – what then is the reaction? I have talked to countless competitors about this sort of thing and invariably found the same answer: that these are not difficult obstacles and it is a matter of taking them straight and clear. For the most part they look so obvious from the saddle that neither horse nor rider have any doubts about their position and sail on. But there would be most awful difficulties if made of light and flimsy timbers. Clearing a gate or a big farm wagon is actually easier and more direct than, say, a zig-zag of rails. Most of all what matters to the horse is the groundline or baseline to an obstacle highlighting the take-off point. The Trakehner type of obstacle can be difficult in this respect because it often casts a confusing shadow. Riders and horses prefer filled-in fences, where brushwood or other materials are used, because they put a bottom in the obstacle. Burghley has always had a favourable reputation for its Christmas tree bottoming. Places that are wide open without a groundline can look easier to spectators than to horses, and riders certainly know this when they walk the course.

About halfway round on foot one begins to feel somewhat leg weary walking the course, unless remarkably fit, and that is actually a good thing. It serves as a reminder that having done roads and tracks and steeplechase plus the obstacles on course so far, our horse will be getting more than a mite weary. This is where condition and all other factors must get computed and further obstacles assessed in the knowledge that the next day the mount could be somewhat weary and not up to the performance and speed of one fresh out and going like a train. Of course one should not be guilty of under-rating any horse that is well-prepared and in top order. If the ground is good then it should be up to this trial and complete without recourse to tactics which will save his legs. It's simply a matter of being prepared for any mischance. This happened at a recent World Championships in the USA where the best internationals assembled in great order only to have terribly difficult hot weather conditions and hard going to contend with, so that many were not acclimatised and, over a massive course, simply dragged round to the point of collapse. This illustrates the point I am making in that the unexpected can happen and take its toll. Some experts commented after that near débâcle that riders too often sat back and pushed their mounts on regardless, taking short cuts for speed and finishing with time in hand. If that really was the case then it gives us a lesson in tactics: spare the rod, spare the horse and nurse it round for a well-timed finish. That is more like the way to take an endurance test than pushing on regardless, because, as we've noted before, there are no prizes for finishing early.

Knowing the course and its hazards is one thing; knowing the route of the course is another. That may sound odd, yet when you think of it there is a lot of country to cover, with many tricky twists and turns, and so it is quite useful to be familiar with the general route that must be taken, especially when a mistake could cost 20 penalties, if not Elimination. Fortunately there is a standard system of marking the course and let me explain this in full detail.

Red or white boundary flags are used to mark start and finish and compulsory sections of the course, to define obstacles, and indicate compulsory changes of direction. They are placed in such a way that a rider must leave a red flag on the right and a white one on the left. Rules emphasise that these red or white flags must be respected, under penalty of Elimination, wherever they may occur on the course, singly or in pairs.

The word 'compulsory' there is a bit confusing, but means just what it says; there are no alternatives. Only obstacles numbered and marked by two boundary flags are judged as such and where there are alternatives the boundaries of each may be flagged red and white.

Direction markers or signs are normally yellow and simply show the way along the course.

Coloured indicators are used to differentiate between classes. Blue may be used for Advanced riders, green for Open Intermediate and Intermediate, and yellow for Novice classes. Sometimes more than one class goes over a part of the same course but in that event it will still be clearly marked.

Nothing is more tedious than being penalised for taking a wrong course, infringing a penalty zone by circling or some similar action, or getting the wrong side of a flag. It does happen and it is simply due to the efficiency of course markers that it happens so infrequently, because it is only too easy to go wrong when concentrating on riding. The more so if you've taken a fall earlier and are seeing stars as well as obstacles and markers!

Now take it that you are riding the course and going well and then for various reasons you get into difficulties. What happens? Usually control is so efficient that following horses are stopped, but according to the Rule if about to be overtaken by a following competitor the combination in difficulty must clear the way quickly. Easier said than done, no doubt. In fact stoppages on course are not infrequent and procedure is for time stoppages to be recorded in case of subsequent objection being lodged. It is without question a disadvantage to be halted, but there will always be occasion for it and so stoppages must be taken in good part.

Where a competitor gets eliminated on course the proper procedure is to retire at the walk and take every precaution to avoid getting in the way of others on course. Unlike show-jumping it is not permissible to take a further fence to restore confidence.

One factor really beyond control and which may come as something unexpected and startling is that of the crowd thronging the popular fences and places such as the water splash. Worse, perhaps, is the sudden sight of people crossing the course when one is galloping headlong towards them. Fortunately it often looks worse than it is; indeed crowds are remarkably well attuned to horse trials considering their lack of knowledge. They seem to get caught up in the atmosphere and enter the whole spirit of the thing. As a result when the Steward blows a whistle and calls 'Horse on course', people rustle themselves into order behind the ropes and await the arrival of the next competitor in expectant silence. Only after the fence is safely negotiated and the combination receding into the distance does a flutter of approval or applause break out. There are, of course, exceptions, but mounted hunt staff and numerous attentive stewards do seem to keep control, even when some 150,000 people may attend a major three-day event.

They say that the most welcome sight of all to cross-country riders is the final fence, and clearly most enjoy the final gallop in as they gasp with relief and pent-up tension. For even the most experienced it is a major test, but after a fall or two, a refusal and some hairy moments, getting home is something special. Yet don't go away with the idea that neither part of the combination really enjoys it, for this is not the case. Goodness one finds competitors coming back year after year and never even being placed at that. The secret is in the excitement a good course offers a first-class horse and rider and it is a great experience simply to get round. Certainly it is difficult, nerve-racking, and even risky, but isn't that a combination of just the things which make up a challenge? And after doing it the sense of fulfilment and the knowledge of having had the guts to go on is simply tremendous. There is one other thing which is seldom mentioned but should be – that horse trials competitors enjoy a great camaraderie amongst themselves and with the officials which goes far to relieve tensions and resolve disputes, and unstintingly help each other in difficulties. Now that is the spirit of sport!

There is one other action to be taken by the cross-country rider on finishing this phase – the weigh-in. This must be done the minute a rider finishes when he dismounts only on the order of and in front of the Steward in charge of that operation. Failure to comply means Elimination. Competitors must weigh-in, if necessary, all saddlery (less bridle) and without a whip but if under weight the bridle may be added to saddlery. The minimum weight to be carried on the cross-country phase of Advanced, Open Intermediate and Intermediate classes, whether in one-, two- or three-day trials (excluding juniors of course) is 165 lb (74 kg) and a competitor under weight is eliminated. As with other equestrian sports, lead weights may be carried in order to satisfy this requirement, but naturally deadweight of this nature is never wanted, so lightweight riders can be disadvantaged.

Within about half an hour of completing the course a competitor's result will be put up on the big score board giving a breakdown of time and jump penalties with the totals incurred. This gives an overall result in the case of one-day or smaller trials and for the longer ones gives a very good indication of the likely outcome. Even so there is more drama to come with the 'morrow's veterinary inspections and then the final show-jumping phase. Some pundits infer that this scarcely matters and that after Phase D it is virtually over. The following chapters take a rather different view, which I feel is justified and adds to our conclusion that a horse trials is a well-rounded and complete test.

6

The Vet's Inspection

The end of the cross-country is the beginning of a further test of nagmanship, in the sense that expert attention is often needed in order to restore the horse's vigour and ensure it parades sound the following morning. I made reference to veterinary inspections earlier, and decided to slip in a short chapter on the subject at this point because lots of people attend the final examination in the stable yard but perhaps without much idea of what is involved.

Actually it is quite interesting and something of a phenomenon that there is a keen following at this point of the trials. It need hardly be said that it is an official and crucial part of the proceedings, appearing in the programme. The basic idea is to parade the horses, each in turn walking and trotting up, so that the two veterinary surgeons or inspection panel can assure themselves that the animal is sound enough to continue into the final competitive show-jumping phase. Simple enough one would think, almost routine in fact. That simple statement, however, disguises the amount of work which may well have to go into the horses in stables just in order to stay in the game.

There tends to be something of a social occasion about the veterinary inspection, and this is particularly evident at Badminton where the Queen and her house party almost without exception attend and take a lively interest in proceedings. There can be quite a crowd and nowadays even the television cameras take notice of this happening too. The buzz of animated conversation heightens with the appearance of each horse, so that one can almost gauge the veterinary decision by the onlookers' exclamations, especially when a fancied combination appears to be uneven in their display. And there will be a positive jostling for position when a faller the previous day comes out and attempts to prove that it is fully restored. The public have a remarkable eye for detail and corporate conscience in such matters which one commends in this company but anywhere else would seriously doubt.

What scarcely any but those directly involved know about this inspection is that problem cases have probably been worked on all night, and indeed from the moment the rider weighed-in after cross-country, trainers, grooms, veterinary opinions and others will have been working full out for restorative treatment. Even a fit and superbly conditioned horse is tired after the sort of endurance test given in a major three-day event. It will be taken directly to its box and given a full and detailed examination for injuries and knocks, and it will be cooled and dried off as safeguard against chilling. No more than a light mash or short sustaining drink would be given at this point because rest is the first essential. The feed comes later when the horse is easy and begins looking for it.

A horse which has taken some knocks will probably want veterinary attention, to make sure that these are localised and do not result in unsoundness and too much stiffness next day. The application of fomentations and healing ointments can work wonders if done timeously, and it is a matter often of taking the heat out if puffy or applying heat if there is stiffness there. If one were able to see behind the box doors there would be some surprising scenes revealed! Grooms have been known to work all night long renewing ice-cold bandages and often heat treatment equipment or intravenous drip is called into operation, or injections given to kill pain providing the current Rules allow it.

In most cases, fortunately, straightforward good stable management will work wonders. The right feeding, treatment to local bumps, and a good rest are all that are needed, if followed by early morning grooming to massage those tired muscles and loosen them up. Feeding will have helped restore energy loss (and all sorts of restoratives including milk, eggs, and stout are used) and a walk round will help to reduce some of the stiffness that is there. Needless to add the feet will have been gone over carefully. Turnout can be helpful at inspection, even if it does not exactly deceive the panel in the slightest, but it is good for morale and a smartened up horse always seems better than one dragged out with straws sticking to the mane.

The actual inspection is a commonsense affair, and should be treated as such. No-one would seriously expect a horse at such a stage of the competition to come bounding out and as it is not being paraded for sale, it need not be urged along to give the crowd a display. Try too hard and there's a risk of something giving. They do say that the wily hands with a suspect horse will hold its head up shortly so that it does not nod, as is the wont of one going lame or feeling a foot.

Panels are usually very fair in their judgements, and after all would scarcely risk spinning or turning down a horse well in contention for an award, before such a crowd of onlookers, if it had a reasonable chance at all of making its way over a relatively simple set of jumps to finish. They will act, however, in the kindliest way if they think there is a risk of breakdown and the horse's being unable to make a further phase. And that is as it should be. A further point is that it is well-known that they stretch a few points over the odds in the case of international events where a team horse has travelled across continents to compete. That is also reasonable when one considers that at that level there is often a complete back-up team of experts from the country concerned with a responsibility towards its representatives and they would be unwise to field an unfit horse and risk a breakdown. At least so one would think, but it has to be admitted that such are the pressures of international reputations in sport that many will go to extreme lengths to stay in the contest. They can be thankful then that veterinary panels will act to save them from disgrace at least.

So we have the picture of a rather reduced field still in contention after the Eliminations and trials of cross-country. Those that remain are stiffish and slower, but for the most part still looking very good indeed. This is what it is all about, remember, and if they have the condition and stamina they will be showing it. It is good to see the horses stripped and run out in-hand in this way, looking natural and so easily assessed. When they appear again it will be for the official parade of competitors in the main arena, and that is the prelude to the final show-jumping phase.

We'll follow that one through next.

7

Show-jumping

The final phase of the three-day event, which usually comes before cross-country in lesser trials, is the round of show-jumping. This is what tends to cause confusion in the minds of the general public, who understandably enough can see no difference between this and the other branch of equestrian sport. Efforts are attempted at avoiding such confusion, but the fact is that this particular test is over a set of show-jumps and under the Rules for judging which are set by the British Show-Jumping Association, and so I take the view that this is simply what this phase of competition consists of and indeed that it is a further and conclusive test of the abilities of the combination in all-round equestrian skills.

In the British Horse Society's view the objective of the third day's jumping test is solely to prove that, following the severe test of endurance on the previous day, the horse has retained the suppleness, energy and obedience necessary to continue in service. I do not altogether hold with that as a definition, and in any case since show-jumping is common to horse trials of one or two days, or at Junior level, it is obvious that this phase fulfils a more definite purpose. Show-jumping cannot be compared with the jumping necessary to clear the obstacles on the cross-country course, and it is different in the requirement of a slower pace, tighter turns, and much more accuracy. To put it in simple terms: a strong horse can surmount a cross-country obstacle with a combination of speed, courage and brute force; the same tactics applied to the show-jumping course would be disastrous. It is a more precise and controlled approach and sometimes the courses are skilfully built and laid out to ensure that a fair degree of skill and training are required.

There is a weight restriction of 75 kilos at this jumping phase and it is understood that the course will normally be comparatively simple and straightforward, bearing in mind the obvious weariness of the horses at this stage of competition. Distance is not more than 800 yd (732 metres). A plan of the course, showing the time allowed to complete it, has to be posted up not less than an hour before the jumping starts, and it can be walked by competitors at least half an hour beforehand. This is always advisable in order to note the layout at first hand, measure strides between combinations, and check over the best route to save time at turns and on the approach to the bigger fences. Usually there are eight or ten jumps, none being over 3 ft 11 in (1.1 metres) high or 5 ft 11 in (1.8 metres) spread at the highest point and 9 ft 2 in (2.7 metres) at the base. A water jump is usually included and should not exceed 9 ft 10 in (2.8 metres). These are all modified downwards for Novice and other events. Speed is from 327–382 yd/min (300–350 metres/min) and can add fractional penalties unless watched.

It has to be said that unlike show-jumping proper, this is a contest as a part of the whole trials. So that this means there is no intention of finding any winner as such and the only tangible results are that competitors are subject to having further penalties added to their scorecard so far. As in the discipline of show-jumping, a disobedience, knock-down, or touch at the water, are all faulted. Whereas in show-jumping these may incur three faults for a refusal, doubled for a second time and eliminated with a third one, or four faults for not clearing a jump, in horse trials it is ten penalties for refusing and five, for not clearing a jump, doubled for a second disobedience and then Elimination. A fall of horse or rider costs 15 penalties (show-jumping eight faults) and every four seconds over the time allowed costs a penalty point. Course errors not corrected can also result in Elimination. There is thus ample scope for loss should there be any carelessness in this phase, and that after all is what it is all about.

It is often debated whether the show-jumping is a really effective phase, and sometimes there is criticism that the course is not big enough to exert its influence. The trouble is that we all tend to forget that it is a part of the overall trial, and if we see too many horses completing without seemingly the slightest risk of incurring additional penalties then we are robbed of the drama of there being any alterations in final placings. There is often a remarkable recovery in the condition of horses at this stage, so that we forget how weary they were at the finish of cross-country and think that they could well have been set a more difficult course of jumps. Either way it is a case of being wiser after the event, which probably indicates that the phase is about right in most instances. On occasions show-jumping does completely catch a weary horse unawares and it pays the penalty. Equally the horse which is impressive in dressage and scrapes through cross-country can be put down here, and just as often the bold galloper so adept at cross-country will be just that bit too impetuous over these jumps and possibly be robbed of victory overall. Which is as it should be, because this is after all an all-round trial and the system leaves no rewards for individuality or flashes of brilliance in certain areas of performance.

From the riders' point of view show-jumping in a one-day or lesser event, following the dressage phase usually, is rather routine and something to be got through before having a crack at cross-country. But when it completes the trial, it does assume greater significance. It may be wondered why then this is not the case with each event, but reflection will show that this would not work unless the programme extended over more than one day. Show-jumping coming immediately on top of a work-out on cross-country would be taxing for horse and rider and the transformation unnecessarily difficult, whereas proceeding from dressage to jumping and thence to cross-country is a reasonable progression.

Procedure is to show-jump either in the order drawn in the case of one-day trials or in the bigger events to jump in reverse placing order. This means that the leaders jump last, giving in effect a grandstand finish to the whole competition. It is at this level that things build into a tense and dramatic situation and the finalists, who have worked so hard to this point, have to face a main ring capacity audience knowing that their horse feels the effects of the previous day's exertions and is not at best form, and suffering their own stiffness and bruises, to say the least. So a bit of preliminary schooling over the practice jump is necessary to get the horse in the mood, and this often means knocking one or two poles before it wakes up to the job. There is much at stake, depending on the margin of penalties spread amongst these leading riders and it may be that one disobedience-refusal or one knock-down could be enough to win or lose, or earn a place and the prestige and prize-money which goes with a major event.

There are countless examples to illustrate that this is not just a fanciful idea, or that this sort of situation is the ideal towards which the sport is constantly aiming in order to produce the dramatic finish. It is true that on occasions a whole event is pretty pedestrian from dressage to the final phase, but not when the organisation is right and competition is top class. Then there will inevitably be some major changes in the leaders, and you will see show-jumping pulling its weight and keeping the tension and excitement right up to the end.

There are some excellent examples which I can quote. Take for instance the Olympic three-day event in which West Germany's Karl Schultz lost the gold medal by taking 20 show-jumping penalties and finished with the bronze third position. His horse, Madrigal, was quite brilliant in the dressage phase with only 46 penalties, which was 20 or more better than most of the leaders. And in cross-country he was equally good, so it was undoubtedly the final phase which robbed the combination of certain success. Equally, however, by going clear and incurring no penalties in this phase that Ed Coffin of the United States on Ballycor, proved to be a worthy individual winner, and indeed finished with a penalty tally 11pts lower than the rest. Or look at the results of a fairly typical World Championship where out of twenty-four combinations placed there were only ten clear rounds in show-jumping, and of these three incurred penalties for being over the set time-scale. Many of the contenders improved their positions here by a place or two in the order but this had been an unusually traumatic trial on account of climate, and even with 20 penalties the best combination (Bruce Davidson of the USA on Might Tango) won with a 27 penalty points advantage. Even more decisive was the influence of the jumping on the outcome of the European Championships at Burghley in 1977 when Britain's Lucinda Prior-Palmer won the individual title by less than 2 penalty points margin over Schultz and Madrigal, a remarkably consistent combination incidentally, and with the West German competitor Horst Karsten and Sioux in third. Both the latter could have won, but in fact garnered 10 show-jumping penalties each.

One big advantage which the show-jumping phase has over the other parts of the trials is that it can be carried out at almost any time of the year on a separate basis, and in practice many of our leading riders make a point of taking their horses out on the winter circuit on occasions, as part of their schooling for the spring trials. This is an obvious advantage, and indeed the top-class riders now spend a part of their time show-jumping in the summer to prepare themselves and their mounts for this phase. At one time this was hardly necessary, and it was just a case of popping over a few jumps to complete the competition. Nowadays, however, it is rather more than that and many of the jumping courses are tricky and twisting, with a need for the horse to be placed just right if it is to have a chance of going clear. This, of course, is part of the test of obedience and suppleness and as such is a worthwhile exercise. Having stressed that there is this overlap, I should make it clear that it is only as far as preparations for horse trials are concerned and very few trials riders and horses are seriously involved in show-jumping as a sport; there are almost no regular show-jumping competitors engaged in horse trials. It is just not their sport, and for that matter the rewards are so low as to make it inconceivable that they would ever risk their good horses in this way or permit them to participate in any form of endurance test.

There are times when show-jumping seems altogether superfluous in horse trials, but at others it is the exact opposite when it sends competitors' final results up or down one to eight places, and with many moving four places it is clearly giving an effective test and is fully justified. Demands for much bigger courses of show-jumps are unlikely to make very much headway, because all the evidence suggests that the course designers have just about got it right now, and inflicting anything more on horses which are at times excessively tired would never be popular with competitors, owners or the public.

The other aspect of all this is that organising show-jumping in this way produces a spectacular finish to a major horse trials, especially an international where the finalists are closely placed and any mistakes in this last phase can topple the leaders. In such circumstances there is a massive crowd rooting for their countrymen who have all the pressure on them to hang on to their favoured positions. There are not so many sports offering this kind of grandstand finish, particularly having gone through such arduous trials to reach this position and everything now depending on horses going clear of the quite deceptively low but tricky jumps. Just touching a pole can be enough to let it roll from the cups and cost the whole competition. And don't forget that the overall leader to this final phase comes in last so that the outcome is unknown until the very last fence has been cleared. Even then, in exceptional circumstances, it can be that the electronic timing will show the round to be too slow and everything lost. If you doubt that, then consider the case of Captain Mark Phillips who won Badminton on Great Ovation in 1972 by 0.65 difference in final penalty points from Richard Meade on Laurieston, who had up to then led by 0.6 advantage. Forced to go for a clear round the combination were just too slow about it and the marginal penalty points were the result – they were beaten by the clock. Now that is the sort of result which makes for spectacular sport, and since it happens quite often in horse trials it goes a long way towards explaining the great following they have right up to the end of the contest.

The prize-giving follows immediately after show-jumping in the three-day events and is quite an emotional occasion, not least for riders and owners. It is not possible for even the public to be immune from attachment to favourites over three days of competition, still less for the back-up team of trainer, grooms and helpers, who have probably been involved for weeks and months in preparing for just this moment. If their charge has won then that triumphant lap of honour around the arena at the end will be something they will remember for ever, and even if it has only resulted in a place amongst the great horses they will be well content. Indeed for very many people just to finish with honour is enough and they will be proud to recall every minute of the long drama for the rest of their lives. It is that sort of contest.

8

The Horse for Trials

Thus far we have been concerned with the Rules and actual competition in horse trials, but now it is time to turn our attentions to the principal characters: the horse and rider. I hope it will already be firmly established that I am an admirer of both, and indeed feel that they have something a bit special in character and courage; they must have in order to succeed in this triathlon. What we must look at next is the type of preparation which goes on behind the scenes. If we can appreciate just how long it takes to produce a horse (and rider) for this work, the quality and strengths needed, and the schooling and training involved, then it leads to a fuller understanding of the sport.

First, though, is there really anything special about a horse which can show up well in trials? This is undoubtedly a leading question, and it all depends on whether we are thinking of a jolly round, a local Novice trials, or a major three-day event. However, if we take it to mean a horse being brought on progressively to give a pretty fair all-round performance then we know what to expect. The answer in my view is that there may not be anything which may be termed 'special' about such horses, but they must be considered as having that something extra, or above the average run-of-the-mill hunters or jumpers. And, yes, those among the leaders in any of today's keenly contested trials must be considered to be a bit exceptional, while an international winner in equestrian circles has an aura of greatness about it if not magic. Now if you doubt this statement, just go out and try and buy such a horse, because quite frankly they are so scarce and so coveted as to be beyond price. Scarcity and excellence place the best things in that bracket. It can come early in a horse's career, too, because the experts have an eye and a knack for seeing the potential, and competition for these with such promise can take them up to five figure bids surprisingly quickly. The difficulty indeed is to resist the tempting offers in even higher brackets which other nations may make in the hope of purchasing glory for their equestrian teams.

What are the qualities thought to be essential to a trials horse?

1   *Stamina*, which equals endurance and strength. For this there has to be the right breeding background, plenty of strong bone and good growth.
2   *Temperament*, meaning an easy disposition without ill-nature. There are many stresses on a trials horse and if over-excitable it will take too much out of itself as does bad temper and a tendency to get upset. At the same time one would not want the too-sleepy, docile and uneventful type of animal.
3   *Condition*. Now that might be disputed, since this is meant to be built up by management, and it may be better to substitute 'soundness' instead. It comes close to stamina, and yet there is a subtle difference, for there are strong horses which do not hold top condition and those that never quite achieve the absolute peak of perfection in this respect. In trials the horses must do so.
4   *Intelligence* is rarely quoted and 'courage' is put in its place. I believe, however, that these horses are subjected to such intensive schooling or training that it is the elite among them which respond most and this is reflected in performance. It is this response to training which produces confidence and from that stems courage. A bold jumper, for example, is one which recalls its schooling and responds to the rider's signals. Trials horses go much farther in that they draw on experience to get themselves (and the rider) out of difficulties.

I have listed the prime qualities but the interesting thing is that you simply cannot stick a label on a Thoroughbred horse and declare it to be a first-class prospect or potential trials animal. They may look perfection, but there is need here for more than a show quality. One of the most spectacular happenings ever in the, admittedly, short history of horse trials was the major win at Burghley in 1967 by Lorna Sutherland (now Mrs. Clarke) on an ordinary skewbald cob, whose sire was Thoroughbred but whose dam had pulled a cart. Let me add that it was no fluke success and the combination was up against a quality international field. So far as I am aware this is the only record of such a win by a rank outsider which was just not rated, and deserves to be mentioned. I must make the point that Popadom's rider was a member of a notable equestrian family and, moreover, she made a great comeback by winning Burghley on Greco in 1978. Let me add that this horse was quite different and quite fashionably bred. So how could that skewbald cob do it? In a nutshell he had that touch of magic, was rather a character, but above all rider and horse formed a very remarkable partnership. Besides they put in a power of work together and that's something else.

Perhaps I could put that story in better perspective by quoting a different example, which comes readily to mind. It is that of Major Derek Allhusen's yard which has arguably produced more British top-class trials winners than any other. A rider of great ability and member of the team which brought the Olympic gold medal home from Mexico in 1968, when he won the individual silver medal, he bred a line of very good horses of which Laurieston is the prime example. This horse was sired by a Hunter Improvement Society stallion, Happy Monarch, out of the mare Laurien which produced several foals for the stables; yet *she* came from a dam brought home from Germany after the war for about £50. Laurien was a member of the British European Championships three-day trials team in 1957 and won the bronze medal two years later. Allhusen repeated this sequence on Lochinvar, a horse he bought in Ireland and then brought on to win team gold and individual silver medals in the 1968 Olympic Games. Laurieston won Olympic team and individual gold medals in the skilful hands of Richard Meade at the Games in 1972. Now that is a remarkable achievement from one yard, and incidentally there may yet be other representatives to come forward.

How has this been done? I think the Allhusens would be the first to agree that there was the essential ingredient of good fortune in finding a good line of stock, but then selection played its part.

There was equal care in breeding to first-class stallions, and then the young horses were broken and schooled patiently and well. The policy was to ensure that the horses enjoyed their training – jumping naturally and never over-facing them, and also taking care to provide plenty of variety in the programme. The other basic point is that management has always been notable, with ample clean pasture so that young stock have been done well and allowed to grow on steadily without interruption. This helps to develop them and generally they have made a good size for competition stock. A colleague who saw one of Laurien's later foals (Laurieman by Marmont ex Ragusa) reported that at four years old he was still growing to pass his 16.1 hands height and had taken his dam's kindly head and calm and expressive eyes, with a sensible outlook on life that was interested and without fear or flightiness. I thought that was a remarkably good description, and you know it does nicely sum up the sort of qualities we look for in a trials horse likely to make its mark in competitions. It suggests such a youngster will reach a useful height and have the strength and stamina; and we know the stables has the reputation for turning them out right. The horse at four is still growing and manifestly not being rushed on, whereas many people would be impatient for it to earn its keep and have it jumping much too soon. Then that description of an intelligent, sufficiently bold and interested disposition contributes to the qualities or plus factors we were discussing earlier.

Let us look in more detail at the horse, beginning with this question of breed or type. It has been said that the horse to select would be a quality Thoroughbred with bone and enduring speed. Now in effect a TB (or Thoroughbred) is many different things in different places, being developed from the earliest Arabians and with the certain influence of local strains of mixed blood. At the top, for quality and speed, we have the British racehorse, and then you get them coming down the scale a bit – not necessarily in quality so much as purity – with good blood horses of somewhat thicker hunter type and so on. Then there are those with a definite part strain or admixture of types and breeding lines, even with a contribution from heavyweights like the Irish Draught or Clydesdale breeds. These may slow them down a bit for racing, obviously, but they do contribute greatly in bone and strength and therefore to stamina and endurance. Of course the relationship can be a few times removed into second or third crosses, but if it is there on one side at least, then there will be less risk of unsoundness. Those who are unkind to our TB and Arab pure-bred lines are inclined to suggest that they are lacking in substance and brainless with it, which of course is too extreme, but often there is some substance in the most outrageous statements and most people would agree that near or three-parts TB is a better proposition for trials work than the pure-bred. Get them from a stock with a background in the hunting field in the English Shires or from Ireland with its daunting stone walls and the cross-country work comes naturally to them. This is partly because it is in the blood anyway, but more especially as natural selection inclines to favour the type which can perform in such country. Sometimes, too, there is a helpful contribution from native pony stock at some point. There is a fine example of this in Anneli Drummond-Hay (now Wucherpfennig) with the great Badminton and Burghley winner of the 'Sixties, Merely-a-Monarch, whose g.d. on one side was a stocky Fell pony.

There is ever-lasting debate on whether mares or geldings are better for competition work, with most riders agreeing on the latter. The record books suggest that previously more mares were ridden and were winning than in recent years, with Laurien one of the few exceptions and when Captain Phillips on Maid Marion won Burghley in 1973 she became the first mare to do so. Those in favour of mares think them more intelligent and besides, if they do have to be retired early, they can go to stud. Gelding owners assert that geldings are less temperamental and give a longer season's use besides being stronger. The evidence certainly seems to be on their side.

Next there is type, and by now we have a good idea of what the potential eventer or trials horse looks like. It has to be a good specimen, well-grown and strong, without any defects in conformation for otherwise there is risk of early breakdown and unsoundness resultant from the hard training and endurance work in front of it. So the expert looks for the right framework, or what is known as a good stamp of a horse. The overall impression should be of strength and balance.

Whatever we may say about disposition and the rest it is clear that a trials candidate will need these qualities. Age and maturity, clearly, must be taken into consideration, but basically we are considering a four-year-old plus animal. If it is well-proportioned, then balance is improved compared to that which is ungainly, awkward and with particular features over-emphasised. The pundits do say that a slope to the tail and heavy hindquarters denote a good jumper, but the trials horse is an all-rounder and so the right outline is vital. A strong back which is reasonably straight and not too short-coupled is a help to carrying or supporting weight; besides it is less liable to soreness, compared with one that is too prominent, especially at the withers.

The neck is part of the topline really, and the role it plays in maintaining balance is often under-estimated. A good length of neck in proportion to the whole, running smoothly into the shoulders, can help if a horse uses it properly. It is not too thick but should be nice and broad, muscular and with clearly marked jugular and windpipe groove. A galloping horse needs capacity and viewed from the front there must be breadth of breast to give ample lung-space. Shoulders are a moot point, for some like the typical TB type which is narrowish and very sloped and others prefer the straighter version which, when strongly muscled, gives a cart-horse appearance. I'd look for a happy medium in which a measure of pulling power is allied to the needs of the riding horse. There is a saying about having something substantial in front of the saddle, which a too-sloping shoulder does not give. Which brings us to the middle or belly of the animal. Is it greyhound or carty type? Neither would be good in an event. For a start, there has to be a fairly powerful rib-cage, wide and well-sprung, giving the heart and lungs ample room. The lower line or belly always runs up under the belly but preferably not too much. You want a good barrel or girth to an active horse and I have never seen one yet worth much if it had no middle to it. An active horse is a work horse and not an ornament, which means it must move, breathe and feed heartily and actively and it cannot perform these tasks without the right conformation.

The drive comes from the horse's quarters or hind legs and so they must be strong, well-rounded and muscular and with some breadth there. As indicated, this is not supporting the extremes of all buttock and no forehand, but strength there in keeping with the rest. The tail is never mentioned but we like to see it correctly set as an indicator of good quarters. Now all experts concentrate on the legs or their action and this is why the judge or assessor at inspection spends so much of the time having the horse walked out in front of the line of vision and trotted back towards them.

See the way the feet are tracking up i.e. hind hoof going virtually into the mark left by the fore hoof, moving in a straight line and not 'paddling' with a good brisk stride. It pays to watch a horse's feet in action as this tells quite a lot about it – whether sound and in condition, and just how good a mover it really is. It may be rather quaint to hear people say they like to see a horse four-square with a leg at each corner, but it is descriptive. What is not liked is one with legs too close together, where conformation is patently wrong and balance and stride likely to be affected as a result. It is fashionable, too, to deplore the lack of bone which is very much our concern since the flatness and density have a direct influence on future soundness, while the strength associated with a good proportion of bone is related to the endurance qualities. Then we also want a good set of feet, remembering the old saying 'No foot, no 'orse' which is very true and one that gets a good grip of the ground from a broad well-shaped foot invariably goes well. The pastern or fetlock does not want to be too much sloped, nor yet too upright, because that in between wears best.

Some experts scoff at ideas that a pretty face has anything to do with the value of horse to rider. Nonsense! All the character is there and a good head to a trials horse is important. Physically it needs broad nostrils and muzzle for breathing and feeding, while well-set eyes that are honest and clear and well-cocked ears are signs of intelligence and temperament. One seldom sees the horse with a wicked eye, ears flattened back, and every sign of unwillingness getting far to the front in competitions as varied as those we are discussing. This is not to say that we would expect a docile and dreamy sort; that would be lacking in character and ambition.

Finally there is the question of overall fitness, and here the best types will fairly dance about with vitality, having a bright gleam to a healthy and glowing coat on which the skin is elastic and ripples with movement. The eyes are clear and bright, feet hard and muscling all over firm and athletic. This is the sort of picture we want of the potential eventer. Many are advertised as such and few ever make it. Keep this ideal in mind and when next at trials compare the horses for yourself and see how many match up. I am confident that those coming closest will be well up the results board.

9

The Training Period

Assuming we now have this ideal type of horse, about 16 hands high and five or six years old, this will be a more than useful candidate for competition. Having been carefully broken to saddle and brought on gradually and sympathetically, it will be ready for the next stage of education and will respond readily enough providing this is kept interesting, varied and the work is not overdone. It is surprising how many people think a young horse never lacks for energy and can and should work all day – and so very wrong because its energy is often still being spent on growth, its bones are still soft and overdoing things can be damaging.

The lunge rein is an ideal starter and fifteen or twenty minutes a day being handled from the centre of a schooling ring unmounted and controlled by this long lead attached to the bridle noseband, can be invaluable. While especially useful in these early stages it continues to be used to work a horse in and for exercise and will be seen at most competitions as horses are warmed up for their work. A long schooling whip and careful handling on the lunge-line will keep the horse working up and developing a degree of collection and using its hocks. We work on either hand i.e. in both directions to develop the muscles evenly, working consciously on improving carriage and balance, and also developing obedience.

Some experts believe in really intensive work, often sticking to the lunge exclusively for weeks at a time, but the better way is to vary things and keep the horse interested and learning constantly. This means regular riding, but not always doing the same things and with the need to develop a good rapport uppermost in order to make steady progress. The one thing that should not be done is incessant work at dressage or jumping, because in the first it is too soon and an awkward, unbalanced youngster is not fit for it, and in the second, excessive jumping, and especially over-facing with impossible obstacles, will probably result in refusals – and who could blame the horse. Patience is the main ingredient at all times and I cannot imagine anything worse than loss of it, after having put a youngster to a big fence at which it quite rightly baulked.

Of course there is nothing better for the up-and-coming trials horse than experience in the hunting field. This, after all, is what it is about: taking a line across country, at a brisk pace and going over all obstacles on the way. Here again, however, a sensible approach is best and the horse is put to the sport gently, not getting over-excited and lathering up, nor allowed to go on until stamina is tested to the limits. It is a matter of building fitness, muscle and condition, and expending energy in a controlled fashion, otherwise the young horse will simply go wild with excitement, be beyond control, and run itself into the ground. After a season's hunting, however, it will have come on to the point where most obstacles have become familiar and if not close in touch the horse will be there at the 'Going home' call.

Of course it is not all play, and there should be a continuing programme of work on the lunge, being ridden in the schooling arena, and roadwork. The build-up is gradual but fairly constant and the aim should be directed towards an outing or two, to one-day trials in the first season after a winter's introduction to hunting, and steady but not too demanding work. The first Novice trials will be little more than schooling sessions, but they still require about three months' careful preparation building from one hour a day to two and a half hours, of which there will be about half an hour's regular dressage training and a gradually extending distance of roadwork which contributes so much to fitness. On top will be varied exercises, popping over a few jumps, cavaletti, or striding over poles, and the occasional short burst at a gallop to open the wind-pipes and relax. If you imagine, however, that every trials horse is made fit by galloping ever-increasing distances then you are mistaken because that would be taxing the strength needlessly. The idea is to build up fitness to the point where the short gallop takes so little out of the animal that it is manifestly capable of going on over the distance without ending up heaving its sides.

The dressage has to be worked on and what the spectator sees in the arena is the result of weeks of practice on the part of horse and rider until the combination is 'word perfect' and the routine flows naturally. First the aim is to get the horse responding to the aids or signals of the rider, to be obedient and become balanced in hand. With that goes forward movement in a straight line and then progressing to good bends on the corners and circles. Then the transitions walk-to-trot, trot-to-canter and so on, upwards and downwards, until the change is barely perceptible and there is no resistance to the request. Anyone who has undertaken extensive courses in riding tuition knows that for rider as well as horse this sort of education is pretty basic, but the difference is that the young horse is being schooled on to compete at a high level and its work must be as near flawless as possible. That requires patient understanding and continued progression to the more advanced movements.

When we watch the dressage tests being ridden we see the end result of all this training. The well-schooled horse responds at once to the rider's aids which are applied by pressure from sitting deeply into the saddle and squeezing with or between the legs and at the same time taking or relaxing the hands, which varies the pressure on the bit by a simple and virtually invisible flexion of the rein. Change of direction is achieved by imperceptibly taking the leg to the side opposite back to control the quarters and stop them from swinging out, at the same time putting the flexion on the rein to emphasise slightly the new direction of travel. Changes of pace are signalled in the same way, often making use of what is called a 'half-halt' to give advance warning of something happening. This consists of the rider sitting deep and applying pressure and closing the hands very slightly, and then almost immediately removing these aids. This is sufficient, however, to give notice to a horse merrily cantering on that you have the intention of reverting to trot in a few more strides, so that when the point is reached the full transition can be made. It is a bit like touching the brake pedal of the car to slow down approaching a halt sign.

Of course it does not happen as easily as that initially, even these basic movements may have to be taught to a 'green' young horse, and even in one that is older it is a case of rider and horse making a good combination and getting fully acquainted with each other's ways and directions. Quite often, too, there are problems of balance which must be worked on, for there can be little improvement until one's mount is made light to the hand, when it will move more like a ballet dancer than a soldier in marching boots. It is a matter of riding the horse up to the bit, and that is a rather misleading term because it is not a case of hauling on the reins and getting hold of it as some would surmise, but riding the horse forward by pushing on with the seat and legs and taking rein until the horse comes back to the rider's hands which it will do by using its hocks and gradually bringing the head down. Very often horses have their heads held high and are virtually out of control. It is the act of riding them which remedies this and in so doing improves the centre of gravity or balance so that it can respond better and go well. Occasionally, of course, the head may be carried low and there again one does not yank it up by the reins but rides it into a more balanced position.

All the work must be carried out in both directions i.e. on both right and left diagonals and usually there is more resistance to going well on one rein than the other. This is because the horse favours one side and is stiff on the opposite, so that this kind of problem has to be worked on and the muscling developed evenly and no resistances encountered. If you picture the dressage arena with its rectangular shape this pattern is duplicated in the training period at home, with the rein being changed by riding across the diagonal from corner to corner across the centre spot. At other times the horse will be ridden in circles up to the centre-line or half the school area. Another good suppling exercise is serpentine movements either along one side of the school or down the centre of it, making deep bends or loops to achieve maximum bend of the horse giving two on either rein. It will be realised that horses have no great facility to curve the backbone in fact, so that every bend is merely an inclination and the animal moves straight forward. It can, however, be schooled to perform a variety of very useful suppling exercises, including work on two separate tracks.

Now the interesting point of such work is that it is an integral part of most dressage tests and is usually seen as some form of exhibitionism or fancy footwork. In fact it is not, but is an extension of the objective of making the horse obedient and supple, so it is perhaps a happy coincidence that these exercises have developed into rather attractive movements which are certainly a joy to watch when skilfully ridden. Also, of course, the simple two-track or lateral movements such as Shoulder-in, *Travers* or *Renvers*, may be developed into a smooth Half-pass right across the school. Basically what happens, with variations obviously, is that the horse moves along separate tracks for fore- and hindquarters with one leg crossing in front of the other. There is as much bend as possible, particularly in the head and neck, and the rider needs to get the direction and then push the horse on around the inside leg. It looks deceptively easy on a well-trained horse but takes some time to achieve from the Novice and is literally done a few steps at a time. *Piaffe* and more advanced movements do not really come within the orbit of the trials horse but are extensions of the same principle.

The psychology of schooling is quite fascinating and possibly not enough thought is given to this when after all it forms a major part of thinking in other aspects of education. The pattern has to be one of some response being followed by warm praise and encouragement, then leaving that work and moving to something more relaxing, only to return to it and ask a little more on the next occasion. And when things go wrong there is just no point in losing your temper, because that would put training back a long way – so far that you've then to begin all over again and remake the ground. Of course there are times when a horse like any other animal (or human) is simply wilful and refuses to do what it is told, and it is then that a sharp reminder with the whip can be effective. It is better, though, if the rider can get the desired result simply by pushing on harder with legs and seat to demonstrate firmness. If discipline has to be used then make sure that it achieves the desired action and be equally generous with praise. That way lies real progress. Of course there are days when no amount of urging will evoke the slightest response; the horse is just disinterested and has gone sour on the work. When that happens it is a case of accepting it and turning to some other work or a gentle hack just to rebuild confidence and maybe stimulate interest again later.

One hears all manner of stories about trainers using harsh methods to get results, but I will tell you this: they could not achieve anything that way. The best professional method is to work hard and patiently, being firm and also encouraging. This applies especially with trials horses for the simple reason that they have to be competent in all three phases and there can be no half-measures. Quite simply this type of horse has to be good.

Would you think that in dressage walk, trot or canter were the easiest to produce? Watch them in the arena and the answer would be that there is no difference, and if the combination is working well then one movement or pace flows into the next seemingly without effort. Still we know differently. The walk in four-time movement is possibly one of the most difficult paces to ride, particularly when trying to create a good impression. The horse must go straight and still bend at the right points of the arena, and the action will be readily seen as a check on progress. There must be some life about the movement, without once breaking to trot or swinging off the track. Clearly it helps to have warmed-up one's mount before riding the test, getting a degree of collection and possibly taking some of the steam or excess energy out before it boils over and the horse gets unmanageable.

The trot in two-time is easier, although not everyone will agree of course. Riding a sitting trot is preferable when allowed, since this gives closest contact and control. It is important not to create impulsion and speed the pace of trot, when of course what is wanted is a smarter and collected trot. Watch the horses at this pace. It is always interesting, looks effortless and yet invariably the riders are working hard to maintain pace, improve collection and balance, and avoid breaking into canter.

Cantering-on (three-time) can and should come from smooth transition, but usually needs practice because the horse must be bent in the right direction, trained to both, and got off on the right leg. Then it must be got going but controlled. I always think horses in the dressage arena a pleasure to watch at this, especially when compared with those in most riding school classes where they sail off at speed and lack all finesse. The aid or signal for canter is to flex correctly (hands), then use the opposite leg behind the girth lightly as a signal and to stop the quarters swinging out, while the inside leg is on the girth to maintain the pace as necessary. Properly developed, these signals will be effective although barely seen and the well-trained horse will act with the slightest of movement from the rider's legs. We shall look at the rider's role in a following chapter, but horse and rider must always be seen as the one combination.

Good extension is something to which schooling attention is directed, and is not always easy. It comes at a later stage, when the paces and the transitions are known, and what is required next is a development of each pace. This is achieved by creating more impulsion when in collection and ensuring that instead of merely going faster around the arena the horse instead extends each stride. Because it is beautifully balanced it is possible to train to get the legs covering more ground and at the same time being picked up higher to give the impression of the horse striding out athletically and with a marvellously springing step. Not all horses have the same pattern of extension, which obviously varies with conformation and condition, but all are capable of stepping out smartly in varying degrees. And it is always possible to work at this for improvement. Remember that it comes initially from the rider: without seat and legs and hands creating impulsion and controlling it, there could never be extension. Control is very much the operative word.

It may be helpful to think of collection as the gathering up of energy – the winding-up – while extension is the outlet for it, always remembering, too, that it is up to the rider to keep it going for as long as is necessary, being careful to show extension in the right places, or as indicated in the test, with those for canter invariably along the side of the arena. This is something, by the way, which should not be practised endlessly, and the pace must be varied and again ridden on both reins. It is tiring work and there are limits to the production of extended paces over more than a short distance. Initially we look for two or three strides and go on from there.

So far we have looked at various aspects of schooling in relation to the dressage test. Roads and tracks are simple endurance, for which read condition. We must therefore turn attention back to cross-country and jumping, but first note that the training referred to is also the basis for success in jumping. How can this be? Simply because obedience stems from it, the horse is responding to the rider, going straight and learning to adjust strides and pace with some precision. All these things are crucial to success in jumping, and particularly so where show-jumping is concerned over a tight course and twisty track against the clock. Really, jumping is the basic, because work over poles and cavaletti or small jumps, helps teach the horse to use itself, pick up the feet and become athletic. Curiously, it is not the height of the fence or obstacle which is fundamental to success, as some imagine, but the principle of developing a stride into it and above all of being obedient and confident with the rider.

I visited a leading horse trials competitor on one occasion to study his methods in preparation for an event. He had a very good six-year-old gelding that stood 16.3 hands high, and that is just about ideal for trials. Carefully brought on, he had a season's hunting and then the real work of being on the lunge rein and worked by the hour, alternately being ridden in a small paddock and schooling area. What impressed most was the way that ridden work over poles laid on the ground at 1.3 yd (1.2 metres) intervals effectively got the stride lengthened with the horse picking up the feet neatly and being interested. They progressed from this to cavaletti, which are of course simple jumps 1½ ft (0.45 metre) high on x-shaped frames 3 ft (0.9 metre) high with 9 ft (2.7 metres) poles laid across. With a collection of these all sorts of combination jumps can be built up, either singly to pop over as a progression from poles flat on the ground, or built up into a set of three to make a bigger jump. A good course in use on this occasion consisted of a series of poles on the ground, then succession of three cavaletti and finally the jump – all set a horse stride apart, on a semi-circle. Now that pattern sorts out the strides, gets the horse on a bend and sets the simple jump in perspective. It is interesting for horse and rider and achieves all that is required in an encouraging way. Moreover after popping over that layout a time or two it is simple enough to stop and rearrange it and thus make the horse think things out afresh. Further, as progress is made so the occasional question will be slotted into the training session, possibly with a more testing jump placed two strides out from the poles, and then a spread, and so on.

If you get the impression that there is a good deal of ingenuity about all this, then that would be correct because it comprises a progressive course in education in an encouraging way. It is also, and don't forget this, a course in building up physical fitness; if the muscles are not developed and a horse is turned out for competition unfit and stiff then obviously it will perform disastrously, and will probably be put off altogether.

A horse can be handled over poles and a simple obstacle equally well from the lunge rein, and it is obviously useful for the handler to be able to see just how it is going. Once he gets working well a favourite idea is to incorporate a really solid pole jump on the lungeing circle. Something pretty nearly as thick as a telegraph pole that will be easily seen which is totally solid. This sort of obstacle teaches a horse to jump cleanly, for if it attempts to scramble over it will feel the knock and learn a valuable lesson without much risk of damaging itself. They do say that this is one of the most important things that a trials horse can learn in early stages, and that as a result it will sail into obstacles much higher from that point on. As explained in Chapter 2, 'rapping' while a horse trials is in progress or just before it is severely frowned on, but there is no doubt that the method is used in the home arena where a horse is getting too close to obstacles and needs to be taught to clear them at a respectful distance. What I do think is unfair is when a helper takes one end of a pole and deliberately raps the horse by raising it as it goes over. It seems better to let the animal work it out sensibly in practice sessions then failure can usually be laid at the door of the training methods. An honest horse trying hard deserves help in sorting out any problems which arise, and personally I should regard any devious tricks as a breach of the faith which should have been built up between horse and rider and equally of the trainer.

How, one may ask, is a horse expected to cope with the amazing variety of obstacles set in cross-country phases of horse trials? Well, the basis of these is, of course, that he will have gained experience in the hunting field. That is preparation for getting over all manner of different obstacles, except that they are taken in the heat of the chase and in exciting company, whereas in a competition it is a solo approach and individual effort. Don't forget, however, that even in those circumstances a horse has the confidence of its rider and if aimed at something pretty horrendous this factor can make all the difference. The problems that water obstacles present can have been overcome long before the trials dates so that there is nothing startling about them, and it is possible to anticipate a lot of other hazards and work on them too.

Oddly enough the bold galloping horses, which can yet be obedient and responsive in dressage, can often funk the final show-jumping phase. There are no end of useful event horses which lack accuracy at the end, which is rather surprising until we remember that possibly their riders have just not worked on that requirement.

Show-jumps are not solid obstacles and often the merest touch or back-flick of hoof can dislodge a pole from the cups. Accordingly, more accuracy and familiarity are needed with these more open jumps, particularly when it comes to strides between. The remedy is usually to make a point of competing in one or two Novice contests before horse trials season comes along, and indoor arenas are especially useful for getting the tighter turns sorted out. If the competitive round proves disastrous then there is no alternative but to return home and put it all together again!

10

The Rider

Now that we have taken a close look at the most important aspects of the horse, it is surely time to turn our attention to the other half of the combination and try and assess what it is that makes a good rider. In first place I would suggest natural balance, and then such factors as good hands, ability to associate with the horse, plus a sufficiency of plain commonsense, courage and patience. I think that a genuine admiration and love of horses is instinctively associated with all this, and cannot imagine anyone succeeding with them who shares nothing.

Are horse trials riders any different from others? I think not, although there are several different points of view on this one, including one that says that anyone aiming for the highest levels of competition in this discipline must simply look on the horse as the vehicle for success. They must, in other words, abandon all feelings, train ruthlessly, and push them on regardless. This is all nonsense and I don't accept that that outlook is general in the top ranks of the sport at all; nor would it result in any sort of success worth mentioning. Trials horses are much too scarce and valuable, too rare altogether, to be ruthlessly ridden into the ground in such unfeeling manner. Besides such a rider would not get the results from the mount and this need for a sympathetic approach and *rapport* has been repeatedly stressed for very sound reasons. I would not deny for one moment that at the top level of international competition the representatives of some, supposedly civilised, countries take the view that horses are expendable, to the extent that they will carry on regardless even if their mounts had, as the saying goes, 'bowed a tendon' or something similar with risk of total breakdown resulting. This sort of ruthless and uncaring attitude in pursuit of honours goes on in every sphere of sport, but I think that the way horse trials are conducted helps to give us the assurance that caring pays for most.

We must not confuse that sort of ruthlessness with the boldness and courage of the horse trials rider, and I do think that the best are unique in that they have to be first-class all-rounders able to produce a horse well in dressage work and to show-jump accurately. Above all they must have the guts to ride them through the very big cross-country courses which are now commonplace and expected. Make no mistake about it, because it does take courage to ride straight into a massive obstacle. I have known international riders who have shaken like leaves when simply walking or being driven round a course. We've wondered time and again if it meant that they were losing their nerve or taste for the sport, but dashed if they haven't come back and won time after time. It may be that this sort of fear and respect for the difficulties is actually part of the solution to their great success, but certainly it is something of an ordeal every time and the wonder is that their trepidation is not communicated to the horse. In most cases it is not, for the simple reason that the minute they are mounted they lose all jitters and become cool, calculating experts and perfect combinations: maybe the uncertainty springs from being only half ready.

Good riding instruction is the prerequisite to entering any competitions, and absolutely essential to the aspiring trials rider. The grounding has to be right and, while there are always exceptions, it is scarcely possible to be entirely self-taught. The way the horse moves is a reflection of the rider, but alas we cannot see ourselves satisfactorily from the driving seat and it does require the instructor to dissemble on the spot, and even though we can be helped nowadays by mirrors alongside indoor arenas and the use of video-recorders to reproduce our movements, there is simply nothing to beat immediate correction and the constant guidance which a good instructor can give. I have been through many hours of it in riding centres and known the frustrations of being unable on occasions to reproduce the results which the expert achieved on the same horse. There is the absolute insistence on perfection up to the standard set and the agonies of trying to get co-operation from a horse which knows full well there is a chance of getting away with it; but also the very real reward of knowing instinctively when one has got it right. You can feel and know just when the right degree of collection is obtained, when your horse is on the right leg and when the stride is such that it will be placed absolutely correctly for the second leg of the combination. It is as satisfying as the snick of golf club on ball when smacked absolutely right.

Nowadays almost every good riding establishment runs regular weekly classes which take riders through all the basic movements up to Novice dressage tests. Children attending the Pony Club camps and special courses do the same. There is, therefore, nothing unusual in such tests and they contain the elements of good riding. Once proficient, the following step is to do some show-jumping and enter a Novice trials which need not be competitive but will give experience over natural obstacles, as will some days' hunting if this is possible.

What is much more difficult is attempting to bring on your own young horse and it should be emphasised that being a good rider oneself is the first essential. How otherwise can you hope to teach a Novice horse? In early stages of competing it is preferable to take over an experienced eventer – a school master who can help the rider. Then with experience it will be an enjoyable and rewarding venture to work and make a young horse; but be warned that it is not an easy task.

Riding at the level of competing in trials can be extremely hard work, and one certainly requires something of the application and dedication of, say, the long-distance runner, probably receiving more setbacks in the process too. The routine of management and the training programme can be very taxing both mentally and physically, working towards that peak required for the day. It will only be achieved by regarding the work and the objective as a source of constant pleasure and interest; certainly not at all if morning stables and exercise on a cold day are a drudge. The rewards are there – and I don't mean medals or prize rosettes – in working together and feeling the improvement and responses, and in the production of a fit and athletic horse. There is financial investment in making a super trials horse, except that one would never wish to sell, but put against the countless hours of endeavour there is certainly no material profit. What you do gain in passing is the art of the all-round accomplished horseman, with a good secure seat, nice balance and sensitive hands, plus an eye for pace and stride. In addition there is good companionship among fellow riders with similar ambitions, and in this discipline they tend to be worth knowing.

One problem which can arise is that of getting and keeping fit if the intention is to ride in horse trials. Now one would imagine that riding exercise alone would ensure this, but it is not the case and with an arduous trial ahead the rider has to work on this along with the horse. A good many turn to yoga exercises, while others to regular jogging or skipping, and include swimming in the routine. Exercises, of course, are also useful and a daily routine can be most helpful. Where there are weight problems then this has to be taken seriously because a combination does not want to be unnecessarily overweight and the less the horse has to carry over the course the better – besides it does not go with peak fitness. Therefore diet may have to be watched too, and indeed trials competitors are as careful about this as are athletes.

Working on steady improvement of riding ability is one aspect, while personal fitness is another, and there is the further need for the development of the intellectual approach to the whole business. There is the need to know the Rules, to plan tactics and time-keeping, and to study each course and each individual obstacle and jump until the questions asked have been answered in the mind. All this has to be related to the horse one is riding, its state of fitness and the weather and ground conditions, to the first-hand accounts of how other riders are going and to what final effort may be needed to win. The bigger the competition the greater the pressures, especially where team membership is involved and international honours are at stake.

One certain advantage is in the rider's ability to relax before taking part: not very easy, except in theory. I always like the story of the international rider who spent the morning of the cross-country phase in bed, taking a light breakfast and reading the newspapers there until it was time to be up and away. That suggests to me the right mental approach and it must assist greatly; accept the fact that the rider concerned has a first-class groom, capable indeed of warming up the horse as well as producing it in top order.

This same calm and confident approach could be crucial to success in a horse trials, particularly when the pressure is on and maybe the horse is dancing about just before going into the dressage arena. Then if the rider gets similarly excited confusion will be rife and there is little chance of a smooth test. Or getting flustered on cross-country when one's horse unaccountably refuses at an obstacle thought to present no problems – maybe he spooks at a spectator behind. The only answer is to face up to the obstacle again and ride him firmly over it, eschewing any temptation to whack hard or in any way lose the place in the saddle. It is at such times of crisis that one's training and natural reactions count most, and they can be the means of turning a fiasco into a winning ride.

A point that should be obvious, but should be made all the same, is that the rider never achieves perfection. That may seem harsh but I am sure all would agree, for there is never an end to attempts at improvement and seldom are horses the same two days running, or any one horse remotely like another. Now here you see is the total fascination of this sport, and it is in the constant striving for improvement, for perfection, and for reproducing the best that horse and rider are capable of, that the challenge lies.

I doubt whether a final word about manners is really necessary so far as horse trials competitors are concerned. They tend to be naturally thoughtful and disciplined, with only occasional lapses, for example of bad language provoked by unthinking spectators getting in the way, or misbehaviour of the horse. Surprisingly enough, there are seldom objections raised as to course or obstacles, unless there have really been some severe mishaps occasioning genuine concern.

Finally it has to be said that the best riders today acknowledge to the full the debt that they owe their specialised trainers. The organisation of courses has become an integral part of top-class trial riders' preparations, particularly when there are major international events in the offing, and the evidence that these sessions are of major benefit can usually be seen in results. Younger riders, in particular, are very well catered for and have every chance of going to the top, providing they have the horse to match their talents. Each country has a handful of expert trainers whose own dedication and enthusiasm for pupils is admirable. In turn the riders tend to give them unceasing praise and their fullest confidence, so that whenever anything goes wrong they tend to return to them to get a clinical assessment and sorting out of their problems. Increasingly, too, there are exchanges of experts, so that, for example, British riders get tuition in dressage by experts of the renowned German, or sometimes the French schools, and on other phases possibly from Americans who have particularly useful analytical methods when it comes to cross-country tactics. Similarly British horsemen are in demand the world over, having done so much to develop equestrian sportsmanship and skills.

Riders carry a great tradition with them, and a responsibility, too, once they earn entitlement to wear the flag of their country internationally. As the sport of horse trials increases and commercial interests become more and more involved, we must hope that the spirit of horsemanship aimed towards excellence in riding will continue to stand up to the test.

11

Stable Management

There is some truth in the arguments that horse trials are won not on the course but in the stable yard, and not so much by the riders as by the grooms working behind the scenes to produce a fit and conditioned horse. To which must be added the reminder that very often, to their credit, rider and groom are the same individual and there are not always big back-up teams on duty leaving the occupant of the saddle nothing to do but concentrate on the particular phase ahead.

Stable management is responsible for keeping the horse fit through all the different stages of preparation, and it must feed correctly to produce the right amount of energy in line with the overall programme of work. There is expertise and understanding needed to keep a good edge to a horse's appetite, both in terms of the amount and the variety fed. It cannot be done to a formula, although numerous people produce massive charts as a blueprint guideline to the subject. The old saying is suggestive of the fact that the eye of the master is the best judge, and it is right since the best guide is the clean feeding trough and any hint of feed left or of poor appetite is a clue to different tactics. Similarly there is the physical appearance to follow, the state of alertness and interest, and the watchful eye on a good digestion and regular dunging. These things, perhaps unnoticed and unthought of by the outsider, are the very essence of stable care in which the slightest change calls for prompt modified treatment so that there is no setback to condition or the work in progress. The basics of good food, a warm, well-ventilated stable, ample drinking water, regular grooming and exercise, we can take for granted. It may be useful, though, to give the outline of a daily routine in order that the work involved be better appreciated.

6.30 – 7.00 am: Morning stables
First inspection, tie up and partly remove rugs to give a brush down, pick out the feet, generally freshen up. Replace rugs. Clean out stables and put in new bedding as required, avoiding excess dust. Set all fair and refill water bucket, check box, water supply and feed, 3 lb (1.4 kg) racehorse or high-energy concentrate cubes.

After breakfast: 9.30 am – 11.00 am: Exercise
Clean up, remove rugs and give a light brush-down, check feet and oil hooves, remove any bandages. Tack up for work and in exercise give any necessary protection to legs. Work about 1 hour dressage exercises then hacking/road work.

11.00 – 11.30 am: Grooming
On returning to stables sweated up, the horse will need a very thorough grooming as against the other light brush-overs. If very hot and sticky may be washed down but must be thoroughly dried off. Legs may need hosing if tender or bumped. Very good grooming should include vigorous strapping or body-brushing to promote muscle i.e. similar to massage. Rug up, according to weather, check over stable and water supply; do any routine jobs in yard.

12.00 – 12.30 pm
Feed cubes/oats and give net of hay.

Afternoon:
Tack cleaning.

4.00 – 5.00 pm: Evening stables
Tie up horse and remove dung, give fresh bedding and set fair. Check water. Depending on season whether horse is led out for short spell to exercise or nibble fresh grass, then set night rugs in order as required and feed cubes/oats/haynet.

8.00 – 10.00 pm. Final check
Ensure all is well, remove dung if necessary, check water supply
and feed cubes/oats/hay.

Now obviously there are many individual variations and the
above is simply intended to give some idea of the work routine
involved with a stabled horse. Normally a spell grazing would be
feasible, especially, of course, when not in training and living
'roughed up' and relaxed. Horses do need regular attention and
checking and it is surprising the incidents which can occur in
stables: prompt action averts problems.

It will take about twelve weeks to get a horse fit and in hard
condition from being pulled in off grass – a month longer if there
is a major competition in the offing. The training programme will
vary from a one hour's period initially up to say two and a half
hours, including the occasional gallop, towards the end of the
preparations. Similarly, the approach to feeding will vary with the
work (energy) requirements, varying downwards from an initial
16–20 lb (7.2 kg–9 kg) hay to 10 lb (4.5 kg) and from between
5–10 lb (2.2–4.5 kg) of concentrate up to 16 lb (7.2 kg) and more,
plus any bran or oats supplements worked in for variety. Most
horses are given one rest day a week, as often as not on a Monday
in general stables, when a restorative soft mash may be substituted
for the hard concentrates and the routine kept to a minimum to
ensure relaxation.

A side benefit about all the grooming is that it really does play
a part in producing fitness and the sleek coat is, in itself, a reward
because it is evidence of good condition – an outwardly visible
indication that the pattern of care is right and the horse is thriving
on it.

Veterinary attention is highly pertinent to the production of a
horse trials entrant, not so much at the professional level, although
this is essential in the case of top-class animals at the slightest risk,
but in regular routines keeping constant checks on progress and on
the alert for any malfunction. This is why foot inspection is constant, and whereas the prick of a thorn or similar would cause pain
and inconvenience through temporary unsoundness in the case of
an ordinary riding horse, when an eventer is in training the interruption to the scheduled programme can be critical and even at
an early stage cause abandonment of some competitions. So it is

good practice and sense to keep regular checks on feet and legs, running a hand over the latter for the slightest sign of heat or bruise and working on it promptly. That way there are minimum problems and one is always on top of them. At the same time, if early warning and treatments show the slightest threat of developing complications then the veterinary surgeon is called and again can usually put things right simply because it is a prompt call and not something overlooked or neglected.

One of the greatest fears is an outbreak of 'the cough', a form of equine influenza, which seems to be as prevalent in summer as winter and is very infectious so that whole stables go down with it. Fortunately routine vaccination gives good control and this should not be forgotten. With any forms of stress, such as respiratory troubles or chills, reactions are the same: watch for it, act on first symptoms, stop work. Any strain at such times burns up energy and taxes the horse's reserves, and must be avoided, whereas quick response results from rest and simple care, helping to fight the virus.

Parasites, especially intestinal worms, are a major problem with horses, and regular dosing is necessary in order to keep the worm-count down. What otherwise would be the point in high-energy feeding and conserving energy, only to have it sapped by these blood-suckers? This is one of the basics in management, an essential part of stable routine, and yet it can be overlooked. I have even known owners resentful of the cost of such treatments and inclined to economy on horses expected to put up athletic performances!

People often ask whether trials horses should have all manner of vitamin and mineral supplements, or worse still stimulants of one sort or another. The latter are quite rightly frowned upon; besides they should not be necessary and would act to disguise true performance. Horses do need minerals and vitamins and are all the better for their supply in the form of supplements to feed, licks, or as a tonic, and while feed compounders make all-embracing claims for their products I think average requirement barely covered, although it is a matter for personal preference and judgement. Always, however, the master's eye – or rather the groom's – is the best decider and guide.

Now for mention of a possibly curious aspect of management: that of stable company. The cost of keeping and preparing a trials horse is now such that increasingly people cut back to one animal in stables. This is less time-consuming than a string but in some ways more difficult to manage, simply because it is an individual. It is very important that it has the company of other horses whenever possible, because it will then settle better with them in competition; besides I think this strengthens the competitive instinct although some might take leave to doubt that view. I think it was Lucinda Prior-Palmer, one of the world's outstanding trials internationalists, who once said that the more one humanises a horse the more human it becomes. There is certainly some truth in that and it must be a part of the process of creating a better combination. So time has to be spent with the horse, developing that desired bond and partnership. This must be more difficult for riders who are neither the owners nor the grooms in constant attendance, and yet any problems can be overcome. An example is to be found in Richard Meade, one of the best international riders, with the most memorable Olympics career extending over a number of years with different horses. Sometimes at quite short notice he has been given the ride in a major three-day event and has invariably struck up a useful partnership. Well, of course, the answer is that he is a fine natural horseman, expert enough to be able to get his mount out of trouble on a stiff course. That is not everyone's good fortune, so while such examples are interesting they may not be particularly relevant and most of us have to approach the task the harder way.

The blacksmith has a role to play in any bid for success in horse trials, and this craftsman can be most helpful with advice and in ensuring that all is well for the day. Most of us, understandably enough, see the 'smith in terms of being shod, but there is more to his skills than simply that, and foot and leg care comes within the orbit. Certainly it is a help to discuss any problems with the blacksmith, especially those relating to how a horse is going, whether there are any peculiarities of gait and if a horse strikes into itself at times, or anything else. Keeping the shoes in good order will, in itself, help the legs and regular attention is advised, with of course a particularly close scrutiny just ahead of trials.

Finally there is the matter of turnout for competition, and while it involves a great deal of work it is a real morale booster and bonus to produce the horse as well as ever you can, groomed, plaited and trimmed in all the right places. A good presence may not materially improve performance, but I think it helps and somehow it does seem that horses know when they are being put on show. They respond in such a way that one can be convinced they really do have a good conceit of themselves!

12

Tacking-up

Strictly speaking the term 'tack' is for horses, meaning tackle or harness, but for this chapter I am extending its use to include the rider's habit as well, because it is of special interest when applied to horse trials. There are three main phases of competition and the practice is to wear riding clothes pertinent to each. A very high standard of dress may be observed and adds at least a few notes of sartorial excellence to these occasions. Better still, riders' various habits underline a note of history, reminding us that these forms of equestrianism go back a long way and tradition is being carried on.

A novel features of horse trials is that the rules specify uniform or hunt dress, plus a hard hat or hunt cap, except that on cross-country a polo-necked sweater or shirt may be worn with breeches and boots and a crash helmet must be worn. In practice, however, riders, themselves, tend to dress up for the occasion and one rarely sees an individual attempting to opt out. It is highly commendable, the more especially as considerable expense and time is involved in conforming to what has become an accepted norm.

Dressage

Military dress uniforms and peaked caps are still evidence of the origins of the sport and army officers continue their support. In three-day trials most civilian competitors wear the classic black swallow tail-coat, once commonly seen worn (also in red) by hunt members in the Midlands of England: very smart too, with double-breasted front and cutaway sides, even if quite impractical. Ladies as well as men favour this coat, and beneath it a few inches of tattersall check or canary yellow waistcoat protrude. Since this is merely the points some competitors have been known to cheat by having a piece of this material only buttoned to the lower half of the coat, thus preserving tradition and keeping cool at the same time. A white hunting stock or tie is worn and securely pinned since it could be most distracting if the ends escape to flap about the head. Breeches are mainly white with black riding boots mahogany trimmed and with white garters, completed with string or soft leather gloves. A black, silk top hat is mandatory, even for the ladies, although they increasingly favour the lower continental version. Spurs are optional and worn curve downwards without rowels, while a whip is another option and may be no longer than 30 in (70 cm). Hunt dress may, of course, be less formal than this but riders in the usual scarlet hunt coats are less often seen than those in the black, which are available to ladies, whereas the more colourful 'pink' is only worn by those daring to cut a dash and emphasise women's liberation. With the black coat plain black boots and garters are worn with buff breeches, even though many wear white breeches and obviously get away with it. With scarlet it has to be white breeches and topped boots. Hunting caps complete this outfit. It has to be added that increasingly there are individual variations, with ladies often favouring blue or brown coats, but for the most part the traditions are followed for the very sound reason that dark clothes compliment the horse and really do contribute something to the overall impression of a smooth and flowing test. Ladies tend to wear their hair up out of the way, often with a hairpiece 'bun' which has become almost part of the tradition. Makeup is done with obvious care, and jewellery avoided.

In lesser one-day trials there is slightly more informality and 'rat-catcher' tweed hacking jackets, buff breeches, black boots and hunting cap may be seen. While permissible, there is no doubt that those more formally attired tend to cut rather a dash and, who knows, maybe steal a point or two as a result.

The cross-country phase is more uniform and less formal, and no matter what the Rules say most riders opt for comfort and avoid uniform or hunting dress. Their appearance resembles that of racing jockeys since coloured silks are worn over the crash skull helmet, which is fitted with safety chin-strap, and with riders tending to favour colours in sweaters or polo-necked jumpers over which are loosely-fitted back and front number cloths. Some opt for nylon breeches but more usually it is standard breeches and boots, matched as before. Some favour hunting stocks minus pins, arguing that they help support the neck, but the loose necks are popular. It should be said that there are no regulations or registration systems for colours which are entirely optional, although it is usual for a rider to choose, and then stay with, the colours and it makes identification easier. Spurs and whips are optional, but usually worn as aids to riding, as are string gloves which give a grip on the rein even in wet conditions.

Increasingly there is a trend to watching safety and ensuring comfort in this phase of riding, and very sensibly too. Many riders wear back supports to protect against serious injury. The use of safety head-gear has been insisted on for a long time and has undoubtedly helped cushion against bad falls. The Pony Club promotes the use of protective hats and chin guards, worn with dark cover over for cross-country and show-jumping and permitting a hard bowler hat or hunting cap for dressage. A tendency for riders to shed all possible weight going across country results in minimum clothing which is not always sensible since clothing can help to absorb some of the knocks. Nylon tights are often worn under synthetic light breeches by both men and women for warmth without weight, and to afford the legs some guard against abrasions which can become very sore. Ancient Greeks of course used to be so proud of their athleticism that they rode naked, but I think today's generation are the better for some protection!

It should be added that cross-country dress is much the same for one-day as for three-day events, and there are very few exceptions on course. It means a big wardrobe case and several swift changes during the day.

The show-jumping phase returns to formality with most men favouring a scarlet hunt coat and the gear which went with the earlier swallow-tail version, except that the usual hunt cap is favoured instead of the top hat. At lesser events there may be more black coats than scarlet, and these are invariably the choice of the ladies. Numbers are tied around the waist as is usual in show-jumping competitions. The Rule states hunting dress which means hunt vest and stock as in dressage and not the white ties and shirts allowed in show-jumping competitions as such.

Major trials finishing with show-jumping automatically have the prize-winners properly attired for their presentation, but it has been remarked often enough in the past that this is not always the case in one-day trials when riders finish with cross-country and promptly change down into something casual and cool while attending to their horses. This results in a rather informal prize-giving which does not please either the organisers or the sponsors – nor indeed the winners themselves when later they see their pictures featuring prominently. Tweed jackets would be the best solution, and yet I doubt if any progress will be made on this one and, rightly, Rules sidestep it.

Having now covered the surprisingly varied changes involved on the part of riders in horse trials, it is quite time we turned our attention to the other half of the combination to see the extent of the tack allowed to the equines concerned in competition, and probably you will be relieved to note that they do not have a different suit for each phase.

Theoretically being involved in several phases of specialised riding would call for a wide selection of saddlery or tack, because the straight-cut dressage saddle which gives more use of the lower leg is not suited to show-jumping where the seat is more forward. This is also the case with the saddle needed for going across country. Much the same arguments could be found to advance claims for most other items of horse clothing, except that there is one cardinal rule which supersedes all others: that the deciding factor will be the tack in which the horse goes best, and which is kindest to the animal. This, after all, goes along with endurance and it is pointless to cut a dash in one arena only to find that the different saddle was not fitting properly and had an adverse effect on the horse's back.

One suspects that this is why the Rules governing horse trials are deliberately framed so as not to make difficulties, because what suits one horse will not do for another and many different circum-stances have to be taken into account. Saddlery is read as the plain English type, which is, in effect, a general-purpose or hunting type and the all-round compromise for our purposes. It has to be a good one, properly fitted and well-used before trials begin, so that it is broken in but at the same time not in any danger of the tree (frame) weakening or stitching coming apart: a happy medium in fact. Similarly, as a horse improves in condition so it is necessary to keep an eye on the saddle to ensure that fit is not affected. Usually a Numnah of sheepskin saddle cloth is fitted beneath to further protect the back, but this should not be automatic and if the saddle is sound it is often better not to follow fashion this way when it may only lead to sweating up. It is not an essential, but it can serve a purpose. The girths holding the saddle in position are key items, especially if one pauses to think of the strain imposed upon these straps in the course of clearing cross-country obstacles. They must be checked frequently for wear as the rider's life can depend on it. For all this it is surprising how frequently girths do break in these trials, which is why a further webbing security strap is often placed over the top of the saddle to support it in case of breakages. Then again many riders fit breastplates or secure the front of the saddle D-rings by short straps to the neck rein of the martingale to ensure that it does not slip back. Rules permit the use of a breastplate or neck rein in all tests. Stirrup leathers are another vulnerable part of tack and again incidences of breakages with resultant loss of balance are not unknown, despite all the checks.

Martingales or any similar device which might be described as artificial aids in dressage tests are not permitted, although they are allowed in later phases if of the running variety. This helps to control the head and while trials horses are expected to be obedient in every respect there is no doubt that over-fitness and an exciting course can produce difficulties which a measure of head control overcomes. The rings are not secured and fixed types of martingales are not permitted.

Now as to bridles, there is insistence on the ordinary simple snaffle for Novice tests and those at Elementary or greater difficulty levels are allowed a choice between that or simple double bridle. Bits may be straight bar or jointed in the centre with eggbutt or bar-type cheeks allowed, but no bit guards or shields. Dropped nosebands to the bridle are often the subject of some controversy but Rules here permit these; and Grakle (cross-over), or Cavesson nosebands are all right, providing they are entirely made of leather and only one noseband may be used at any one time. Blinkers or hoods are banned.

Use of comparatively simple tackle may be described as a feature of horse trials, and very commendable it is too. This way one sees the potential of the combination and it is doubly impressive when the performance does not depend on sophisticated aids, complex ironmongery, or devices which obscure or mask disobediences.

Notice especially in the dressage phase that none of the horses is wearing bandages or boots of any kind, although obviously these are allowed in later phases as safeguards against injury, knocks or the horse striking into itself with hind toes. Any such precautions taken are eminently sensible and may include bandages, leather brushing boots which guard the legs as suggested, and rubber over-boots offering protection for the heels of the forelegs.

Back in stables the horse's wardrobe requirements will be multiplied. This is when the simple approach falls apart and grooms will want a range of rugs, saddle cloths, several sets of clean bandages, poll-guards, different reins, shoe studs, and goodness knows what; besides every sort of grooming tool, shampoo, veterinary preparation and spare parts for all the tack. There is little chance of travelling light when so many eventualities have to be covered!

Finally, let me make the point that tack cleaning is a most necessary chore. When it is being used hard under difficult conditions, it simply must be kept right because on this depends safety, comfort and the whole performance. This is another reason why spares are necessary, otherwise many items will be wet and need thorough cleansing and treatment with time to dry naturally and ensure softness. Turnout in every sense is more than just smartness, although that counts too, but any neglect or skimped preparation of tack may well cost the rider a nasty tumble.

13

The Spectator's Role

At one time, I suppose, it might have been argued that those not actually participating in horse trials were in no way involved; in other words that this was not a spectator sport. The impression could have arisen because of the complexities of the whole thing, and the fact that because competition can be distributed over a very wide area of ground there is no audience concentration. The onlookers appeared thinly spread on the ground, and this could have betokened a lack of interest and enthusiasm.

Well the answer is that nowadays we know better. Horse trials are proving to be the fastest growing area of equestrian sport, and there is great enthusiasm for them, together with increasing appreciation and knowledge of what is entailed and of those taking part. Another important factor is that television coverage has been generous and is so technically brilliant that I for one feel as much involved via the cathode ray tube as when trudging a sticky course as the trials are in progress. It is extremely skilful how television can give us such comprehensive coverage of cross-country phases over all the major obstacles and with repeats where necessary, which enable us to study so much detail. Even when reporting horse trials I have found the cameras the best source of information on course for the simple reason that the individual simply cannot be at every point constantly, and it always seems to happen that one moves on from the water just before someone goes for a swim.

Commentators, such as Dorian Williams and Raymond Brooks-Ward of BBC, have contributed immensely to our enjoyment of horse trials, simply because they are themselves totally dedicated and enthusiastic – they are both, incidentally, Masters of Foxhounds. These internationally-known figures communicate the basics of this sport most successfully to the mass audience in the world of sport and it is not a simple task. There are times, I must admit, when trivial incidents become a bore, notably conjecture on which alternatives a combination are likely to take when we know jolly well that everyone is going for the shortest route home. But these are incursions into the sense of drama and anticipation with which most of us in armchairs can enter into the spirit of the competition. We become involved and sometimes so closely that we can almost feel the bumps, especially when the cameras zoom in to draw us into the saddle. Very welcome, too, have been former competitors' comments as they 'ride the course' with combinations, and none more effectively than Michael Tucker, who rode internationally and owns some good trials horses.

Where television, understandably, fails the enthusiasts is in being unable to take a total view of any event and to a great extent this is an essential feature of this particular sport. We can be entertained and gripped by cross-country highlights, and drawn to the edge of our chairs by the last moments of the show-jumping phase, but snatches are no substitute for knowing the full story. You have to be at the side of the dressage arena at the right moment when a fancied horse spooks or does something unbelievably silly, or conversely puts up such a sparkling test and display of extension that it creates a murmur amid even the hallowed silence of the dedicated. You have to be there to follow through a combination which takes your fancy, because the rider is trying so hard, or the horse's breeding line intrigues, or for any one of a multitude of reasons. Then you become absorbed in the performance of that combination throughout, and you share and get involved in the difficulties of the test. And while there can be only one winner in a big competition there may well be a dozen or more prizes. Any combination which reaches up into higher levels and rides in experienced company can be very well content to finish on any reasonable level of penalty points. It is not entirely a question of competition and winners – do remember it is a trial, or an assessment. There is everything to be said in favour of more frequent reminders on this point, because strictly speaking of course there are no losers at all.

Some years ago I can remember following the progress of a young rider who had a particularly nice-looking horse which he was determined to produce for trials, which were his great interest at that time. Since he was a particularly friendly competitor, never under stress and taking successes or failures as cheerfully in his stride, it was easier than usual to feel involved with the combination. They were extraordinarily smart in turnout and the horse had that extra showy bit of style which could only have come from good breeding that hinted at the best of Thoroughbred with a dash of Arab somewhere along the line. They were a partnership and if either was not on form it showed, but you could always see them working out the problems together either at home later or sometimes on the park. The rider used to work hard in particular at ensuring his horse was not too wound up before competition, talking to relax and usually letting the horse take a bite of grass to achieve this end.

This combination worked on patiently and at length, until the first season approached of being ready for taking trials seriously as distinct from the local one-day pipe-openers. They got scolded for forgetting domestic duties and on an important anniversary had blithely gone on for a schooling session over show-jumps in an indoor arena competition for the experience. They won or were well placed in practically every trial they entered that next season, even if they did have some thrills on the way. It was probably the best-looking and most enthusiastic combination on circuit, and I would say the most sporting. The next year we looked for international rating – which never came and maybe should have done. Anyhow another good spring season was followed by high expectations for a major three-day event. Imagine the drama when this unseeded combination completed dressage in third place and then finished first overall after the cross-country but with the favoured second horse equal on points although so placed as a result of being slower over the course. Accordingly they show-jumped in reverse order and when the other horse put up ten penalties the combination I was following looked certain of overall victory – a notable one too. Alas! They just couldn't put the final jumps together and put up twenty penalties to finish third overall. Still a big success and suddenly the combination was being rated in world terms, being generally reckoned to have flipped in the final due to the strains of being virtually the winners.

The sad sequel to this story is that I appeared to lose touch with the combination after that, idly wondering from time to time whether both were being roughed off until later. Then, long afterwards, I did discover that the horse had met with an accident and had to be put down. It was heartbreaking for the rider and owner, having brought him along from untouched Novice up to the top, and, since he reckoned that you could not find a substitute and repeat it in the time available, there was no alternative but to drop out of the sport.

Now I have given that true story in detail, because to me it epitomises all the ups and downs of horse trials and shows how merely as spectator one can become involved in events. There is fascination and learning about this pursuit of equine excellence, which is so many-sided and seemingly beset with all manner of difficulties and really does require the alliance of skill with luck.

How does one participate in trials as spectator? The answer is to begin by supporting local events, where often there will be well-known riders either giving their top horses an outing or bringing on Novices alongside combinations with much less experience but obviously there for enjoyment. It will be small enough to see everything that happens, or most of it, and you will have the advantage of being up front with the experts and should not hesitate to seek explanation of any points about which you may be in doubt. Do not look for too much sophistication in the way of grandstands, catering-tents, and the rest. Instead take a picnic, a canvas chair, and a pair of binoculars. Stroll around the cross-country course and enjoy the spacious estate grounds in which it is more than likely being held.

A word of warning: be careful not to get in the way, and do avoid getting too close to spirited horses, particularly at their rear end. Children and dogs, especially, should be kept under careful control, because there is the risk of accidents to all concerned. Do not applaud or cheer on competitors in the dressage phase or show-jumping either – you could cause a major upset. Wait until the end and then join in, although actually appreciation is never vocal in horse trials and applause always most restrained. Be especially careful about crossing over the cross-country course when a horse is due to approach. Stewards are there to give warning by whistle and the cry 'Horse on course' which must be heeded at once and the way left open. The riders have enough problems without having to swerve to avoid spectators as well. As spectator interest grows this problem becomes more difficult but with good sense it should never be necessary to impose restrictions, and informality is very much a feature of horse trials.

Always get a programme if it is available, since this gives details of competitors and horses, a plan of the course and events, and often some useful hints on the most interesting or novel obstacles and a resumé of the rules. It often contains the detailed dressage tests being ridden as well. The results as they come in from each phase will be chalked or posted on a big board at a central point and it will add greatly to understanding and interest if this is checked regularly to see how competitors are faring. When they ride the cross-country course there will probably be a detailed commentary so that it is possible to keep a close check on progress from any point.

Be sure to wear stout walking shoes and casual clothing and be well equipped with mackintosh or anorak. A shooting stick is an ideal companion but failing that a stout stick may come in useful for negotiating parts of the course.

I feel it hardly necessary to make the point that spectators will soon appreciate, namely that without the willing co-operation of estate owners providing the facilities there could be no trials. Accordingly, we tend to feel a bit like paying guests and treat the grounds with special care; besides litter could be a fearful hazard to horses. Do please, help in any way possible to persuade others to keep the standards high, if only to ensure we are invited back!

Now there is one final but major point about spectating which we must not dodge, and this concerns the issue of cruelty and harm to the horse. It is always assumed that the rider has a choice, which is why sentiment runs high regarding the position of so-called dumb animals. I must say that I take the view that horses can usually manage to communicate with man very well indeed. They also respond and give as much as they wish in competition – you can ask, but not necessarily get, more. In horse trials there is no denying that athletic performance and endurance (of horse and rider) are tested to the fullest extent, particularly in major three-day events, but the same would be true of any contest at top level and there is no argument but that we do need to test and maintain standards of excellence.

The British Horse Society Rules are quite firm and unequivocal so far as trials are concerned, in that any act construed to be cruel or exploiting the horse will be penalised by Elimination. Similarly if a horse is seen by stewards to be unfit to continue then they have the fullest powers to see that it is taken out of competition. The same applies wherever horse trials are run because these feelings are worldwide and reflected in FEI Rules internationally.

Now this is not to say that spectators can be shielded from seeing horses brought down at obstacles and suffering. Just as riders risk fractures, and the fearful injuries which can result when a falling horse rolls on them, so on occasions are there mishaps causing the loss of the horse. It is an unfortunate fact that leg fractures are an equine disaster, because although with protracted and very costly treatments and operations they may be repairable, the chances of the patient going sound and well again are usually rather remote. In other words a break invariably means the end of an active life for the horse and so to avoid distress and pain it is, or has been, sometimes necessary to summarily dispatch an animal, although one may be sure that this would be done with the utmost care, as well as most discreetly to avoid upsetting anyone. Veterinary science is making remarkable strides though and already there are remarkable success stories of fracture treatments which give cause for hope for the future.

Horses which are frightened and in pain are promptly tranquillised and given injections to mask the injury. What organisers dislike most are the difficulties which obviously can arise through a jumping mistake when the animal is left suspended, straddled over an obstacle. If often looks far worse than it is and again services are invariably close at hand to facilitate rescue. Such happenings are part of the drama of horse trials and inescapable in a living sport, no matter how carefully planned and with entries very carefully screened to ensure both horses and riders have the necessary experience for the tests.

Cruelty sometimes makes headlines and unedifying pictures on the international scene, when possibly course designers and the elements of weather or climate combine to set competitors a really stiff task. Few like this and without fail representations are made by the ruling body of the sport. Invariably the answer is that the trials are at international level and must be tough. It then becomes a matter of national pride to be seen to be upholding the honour of the flag by participating and putting up the best possible result. Sometimes it might be better to retire in protest, but the honourable course is always thought to be to compete, win if possible, and then protest strongly in the interests of future competitors and their horses.

Let us finish on an artistic note. Horse trials offer spectators a fair amount of scope for combining other pursuits and hobbies at the same time and this may be worth thinking about if becoming a regular visitor. Photography offers obvious interest in both the classical airs and graces of dressage and the action of cross-country or jumping. There are also very many unusual candid and amusing shots in all stages. A telephoto lens is essential, because while facilities for amateurs to get close to competitors are good, there will always be better shots out of distance. Painting and sketching can be rewarding in such lovely settings, while there is also time and opportunity to study the countryside and nature at firsthand. Besides, this is an active sport and one in which you have ample choice: follow it at home on television, sit in your own car at the ringside or a vantage point for the whole scene – but better still enjoy the fresh air and a stroll around the course and keep fit too!

14

World-wide

It is often assumed that Britain dominates the sport of horse trials, but this is not really the case and while there is a strong UK tradition, enthusiasm is world-wide. There is evidence for this in the fact that in the major international events an average of at least a dozen countries will be represented, and this is growing steadily despite the obvious difficulties of such keen demand for all too scarce horses at this standard.

The descriptions given to different trials cannot be other than confusing to those unfamiliar with the sport. First, all international three-day trials are conducted under FEI Rules (International Equestrian Federation). Lesser events are organised by individual countries, all broadly similar to those we have been discussing, while participation is carefully controlled.

Major official international three-day events are designated as CCIO which is an FEI phrase or description standing for *Concours Complets Internationaux Officiels* where participation is by invitation of each country's selectors. *Hors concours* or individual entries would not be accepted.

A step down the scale is what is labelled a CCI or *Concours Complets Internationaux* which is an international three-day trial where qualification is by grade and experience and overseas entries are usually at the organisers' discretion and with the approval of competitors' own ruling body.

In Britain the Badminton, Burghley and Wylye trials are examples of CCI status and these can be up-rated to CCIO if, for example, they were invited to hold the European Championships or other major event. The World Championships and the Olympic Games horse trials are classed as CCIO. When the same initial letters are followed by 'J' such as CCIOJ this carries the same meaning, except that they are trials for Junior riders under eighteen years. It should be added that show-jumping and dressage disciplines follow the same international coding systems.

If it sounds unwieldy then fortunately it appears to work smoothly, with the result that world-wide there is good representation which does undoubtedly add extra spice and interest to the occasions.

The Olympic Games is clearly the peak international meeting and has been so since 1912 when equestrian trials were first included. In those days Sweden won the medals and later the Dutch had a run of successes, while Germany dominated when hosts in 1936. Post-war British riders have been most successful, but the USA, Sweden, Germany, France, Australia and Italy have all been represented in gold medal successes. The Olympic Games are held every four years.

World Championships have only been held regularly since 1966, well timed at four-year intervals between Olympics and on the whole not as successful. This is because in a short series conditions have been very arduous and subject of much controversy. Nevertheless it can be argued that they produce some stimulating performances and provide an outstanding elitist platform which has focused attention on the sport, and incidentally produced winning combinations often from countries not winning Olympic medals. European Championships are natural forerunners to both top trials, being held every two years and quite skilfully setting tough courses on the way up to world events.

It is most encouraging to notice that while these big events have by no means been dominated by any one country, there are increasing signs that others not rated at all in the past are now determined on victory. One can point, for instance, to the steady participation and growing successes of the Soviet Union and of Japan, a country not regarded as having a long tradition in equine sports but methodical in the approach, and such as New Zealand which is building teams despite the long distances to travel.

To explore the international aspects of this sport, however, one must look not to traditions or national pride but rather to the small, select and very good company of trainers operating at this level, for they hold the key to any country's progress. There is a surprisingly close-knit affinity between these experts and former pupils everywhere and, increasingly, sponsorship funds are enabling larger numbers to participate and benefit from the equestrian knowledge these men and women disseminate. It is a further explanation for the world-wide growth of the sport.

Who are these trainers? Usually the elite among riding masters, or those who have emerged in the highest ranks of their country's instructor or training ranks. In Britain they have qualified as Fellows of the British Horse Society (FBHS) and in other countries taken a Masters' or Professors' qualification. As such they tend to train other instructors, but may take selected pupils in the higher arts of equestrianism, including dressage and advanced horse trials work. Then again some of the finest freelance trainers are not within the system in so much as they may not hold a qualification other than as an expert rider or horseman but they have special skills to contribute.

For many years Britain's Captain Edy Goldman was outstanding in this field and pupils in many countries worshipped him for what he had given them in a unique way which made notable impact on the then eventing scene. The walls of his office were plastered with tributes and pictures of winners he had trained. Among them were Lorna Sutherland (Clarke), Sheila Willcox, another triple Badminton winner, and a whole string of names which have become synonymous with international trials.

Richard Stillwell is said to be the most sought after instructor in Europe. Based in Berkshire, he spends the greater part of each year abroad, coaching riders making the Canadian, Greek, French, Dutch, and many other national teams. He has had major offers from Middle Eastern countries too. He specialises in short-term courses, solving problems and re-educating horses. The leading lady rider, Lucinda Prior-Palmer, has been one of his pupils, as has Mary Gordon-Watson, World title-holder in 1970, Richard Meade and countless other star riders.

A Swedish trainer, Lars Sederholm, now working in Britain, is a former champion who has developed systematic training which is influential on growing numbers of young riders. He has worked

with many outstanding show-jumpers too, indicating that funda-
mentally the approach is identical. For a time he trained Princess
Anne, former European Champion, whose enthusiasm for the sport
has done much to popularise it. Her principal trainer, however,
was Alison Oliver, who had taught alongside Sederholm for a short
period. They follow similar approaches. Chris Collins is one inter-
nationalist who has trained with Mrs Oliver. Former Oympic
medallist Bertie Hill is another British trainer who has had great
influence on riders, with Captain Mark Phillips an outstanding
example among former pupils, not to mention his influence on
successful international teams.

As might be expected, the USA is a magnet for the world's best
trainers and the country's centre for horse trials teams is in Massa-
chusetts, where former French cavalry instructor Jack le Goff is
the outstanding coach, a man with high ideals and direct style.
He has really been responsible for the emergence of American
riders to the front of the sport and set up an organisation to bring
them on. A single statistic points to his progress, for whereas in
1975 Britain had 110 horses rated as Advanced, in the USA at
that time there were only fourteen. Yet in 1974 the USA took the
World Championship at Burghley with Bruce Davidson on Irish
Cap the best individual and fellow countryman Mike Plumb on
Good Mixture runner-up, and four years later Davidson was able
to repeat his success on Might Tango, with the team third.

Canadians are enthusiastic and useful incentives have been given
to owners to ensure that the best horses are retained for home riders.

French riders have not had the success in horse trials which one
would anticipate, although Jean Guyon won the individual gold
medal at the Mexico Olympic Games in 1968 on Pitou, and riders
have been placed consistently in trials. With the great tradition
of dressage or classical riding at Saumur we expect to see emphasis
on that discipline and will no doubt see increasing interest in trials
before very long. Holland and Belgium maintain a good representation and, judging by the demand for international trainers' services,
are likely to continue to do so, while West Germany has been
remarkably closely in touch with major events in recent times,
suggesting dominance in the future. West Germany has strong
advantages in no lack of the right type of horses in Hanoverian
and Holsteins, and a tradition of disciplined riding.

Russian riders are very likely to present a challenge to the trials world and it should not be overlooked that this country has a fine record in European Championships having won and been runners-up on six or more occasions. They tend to be aggressive riders and great team men, and of course have a good pool of horses in training.

Ireland should do much better in this sport than has been the case, only securing the European title for the first time with the fourteenth event in the series. No country produces more good horses for horse trials, with the Thoroughbred about seven-eighths and a touch of the Irish Draught horse to give the endurance, but they tend to be priced right out of the home market. There are signs, however, that this situation will alter, if only because success in team colours has such a useful effect on the horse trade. The other point is that dressage does not seem to be in character and they are only now working seriously on it with trainers.

Italy is a country producing fine horsemen and this is reflected in the record books. It is worth noting, however, that Switzerland produces some sound teams and they have been in the winning frame on occasions. Scandinavian riders also put up many a good individual challenge, such as that by Nils Maagenson of Denmark to win the European Individual title in 1979 for the first time. Swedish riders have been more in evidence in Olympic competitions, and to great effect too.

With more and more countries becoming interested in horse trials, it is likely that the international scene will be enlivened with more events and existing ones will enjoy stronger support and competition. In turn this will succeed in raising standards, which is all to the good providing that there are sufficient quality horses to go round and they are not over-taxed. The other essential is that nations should follow the spirit of the Olympic Games and of sport in general, enjoying friendly competition and fellowship rather than getting involved in national politics and determination to win merely for these ends, which would be totally disastrous. Running horses in trials is very costly, and there is a tendency for some countries to subsidise with State aid merely for political reasons, which has unfortunate consequences and in fact reduces participation since those without support simply cannot compete. There is, too, this vexed question internationally of riders who are professionals and earning a living and those who are amateurs and paying their own way. It is encouraging that horse trials has not been as much bedevilled by this as, for example, show-jumping has been, but it will certainly require careful control to avoid such problems. Fortunately – or unfortunately some may say – this particular sport offers modest rewards and seems likely to be unchanged in this respect.

Sponsorship is an important factor, right across the world, and the injection of money by commercial organisations has transformed fortunes and also done much to help finance competitors and teams' expenses abroad, as well as fund the training of young riders in regular courses under top instructors. This source of finance is one explanation for the growth of the sport and expansion of spectator interest, since accompanying media publicity and promotion is all part of the package. In Britain, as the home of the sport, there has been outstanding contribution and involvement on the part of Midland Bank and its associates, without whom there simply would not be the present wide programme of events. Similarly Whitbread brewers have sponsored Badminton trials generously as have Raleigh Industries those at Burghley, and the same pattern prevails elsewhere. The Olympic Games, of course, are hosted by different countries and teams are supported by local appeals' funds.

The one major problem with international trials tends to be that of climatic differences, with countries with extreme conditions keen to host competitions but presenting those from temperate climates with special challenges. It has to be said that, as with other sports, there is no reluctance to take part; indeed the problems seem to be successful in stimulating interest and also presenting veterinarians with new insight and so possibly benefiting horses the world over in the long run. However there have, on occasions, been some harrowing trials with competitors (human and equine) clearly exhausted by their tests under the unfamiliar conditions. Either there will have to be extended periods of acclimatisation before the trials or modified cross-country and endurance courses, perhaps even handicapping on national climatic variations, or simple commonsense must revise time-tables and courses in the light of any extreme conditions. One suspects that these could be exploited, which would have nothing in common with the spirit of international horse trials – nor would it prove anything.

There will always be differences of approach internationally, and welcome too since much can be learned thereby, but the basis must be the complete and fairest trial of rider and horse. And to those who complain and would like to see all manner of bans imposed on the exports of horses and sometimes of trainers too, the short answer is that international exchange and trading is a most welcome and necessary feature of the sport. The world grows smaller and competition more intense, but it also offers more frequent and regular stimulating exchanges and challenges.

15

The Organisers' Trials

Whatever your interest may be in horse trials it is not altogether a bad thing to have some knowledge of the organisation that goes into the event. It may well be that at some time your enthusiasm will be directed towards giving assistance, and why not, when it is a first-class way of participating directly and thus helping to provide the facilities needed for up and coming competitors at all levels.

There is a need for superb organisation in this sport and a precedent has been set for it, thanks to the liaison work done by the central body, which goes a long way towards ensuring that standards set are maintained. This is particularly valuable in that it ensures a certain uniformity of test, which is highly desirable. Still a lot can go very wrong unless the organising committee is well chosen and puts a fair amount of planning into the arrangements.

It must all begin, of course, by selecting the right site for trials, although to be honest there is not often a choice and so the question must be asked whether that which is available is right for them. Is it well sited in terms of approach and traffic arrangements, reasonably flat access, but well-drained and with ample car parking? Then the location and suitability of areas for the dressage arenas and show-jumping must be looked at. There must be a fair bit of old, hard-wearing, but good turf there, as flat as possible, even if it is desirable to have the cross-country undulating a bit, with plenty of natural obstacles to work on. Ideally these should have a steepish bank, various ditches, a patch of woodland, and water which is all the better if it affords a bit of a splash without being in any way deep or dangerous.

Initially at least it will be a Novice event although for the present purpose we may as well think of it in terms of a more ambitious one-day programme. Begin by establishing quite clearly the pattern to be followed and allocate each member of the organising committee a positive role, a job to do, or area of responsibility. Ensure that there is plenty of time for preparation – a year is not too long, especially when there are obstacles to be built by volunteers. Get the course designer to work first, producing a rough sketch of the whole area and giving an idea at an early stage as to layout and the sort of obstacles he or she has in mind. Then walk the whole thing several times and plan it on the ground.

We might take the various headings and simply follow what is involved as follows:

Programme

This has to be carefully planned, with particular regard to the time-table. It is not too difficult in the sense that we know the time allocated to each competitor in the various phases, but allow ample time for stoppages, late starts and so on. Decide what entry can be handled and note that it is likely to be over-subscribed so agree the basis of acceptance i.e. first seventy or ballot. If printing a programme, include the plan of the course and as many details as possible for the benefit of spectators. The person responsible can also handle publicity and sell advertising space etc. Make sure the trial dates are circularised well ahead. Invite the local press and keep issuing releases about notable entries and similar news items.

Car parks

Plan access to the ground carefully and consult the police for approval. Arrange signposting with motoring organisations to avoid confusion on roads. Ensure that there are ample attendants in car parks, also a stand-by tractor unit in the event of the field turning sticky and causing problems. Fill up the gateways with hard core.

Catering

Contact caterers well ahead and agree terms in writing. Do so on the recommendation of someone with experience of the firm to ensure that the standard is satisfactory. Negotiate terms and check prices. Make sufficient provision, including a licensed bar if possible, and perhaps several units for snacks at different points. Site catering tents carefully, preferably away from competitive areas. Make suitable provision for entertaining sponsors and guests, and getting snacks out to judges and officials on the course. Choose a secluded site for toilet accommodation and give thought to hiring portable units.

Ground

If plans are prepared and supplies obtained in good time it should not take too long for the official concerned to set up the outline in the few days prior to the trials. Plenty of help will be required, plus tractor and trailer and fencing tools. Use tapes or string on light stakes to mark out the cross-country course, flagged in accordance with Rules. Mark Start and Finish clearly and provide a weighing room hut and scales. Mark out reserved sites for each fence judge, time-keepers etc. Mark out dressage arenas (usually more than one required allowing thirty-six competitors to each) and use rope and sturdy posts to ensure spectators do not encroach. Set up standard letters and markings. Top the grass if very long but leave enough to withstand wear. Provide an area close at hand for competitors to use to ride in their horses. Show-jumping requires an enclosure of about 100 × 80 yd (91.4 × 73 metres) roped off and level with a good sole of turf and preferably suited to ringside cars being parked around three sides (more revenue). Course to be pre-planned and jumps can usually be hired from BSJA local branch.

General

Consider insurance and make public announcement in schedules etc. of disclaimer as to liability. Appoint hon. veterinary surgeons, a doctor and first-aid facilities and make full and adequate provision for emergency services to cover farrier, police, fire, ambulance, trailers for injured horse (with winch), fence repair squads equipped for wire cutting, releasing trapped animals or rebuilding obstacles etc. Provide covered vehicles, tents etc. for judges and time-keepers.

Control

Secretary or Clerk of Course should have separate tent or office accommodation with adequate help, coping with declarations, results etc. Public address equipment is most desirable and for preference there should be links between Control and various points on course. A central score-board should be a prominent feature with results kept up to date for spectators to follow.

Helpers

Each committee member should be responsible for sector organisation and allocated sufficient officials and stewards. These will include the following: announcer, ring stewards on each phase, starters, time-keepers, fence, dressage and jumping judges, arena parties (to replace jumps), gate and programme sellers, car park attendants, messengers or runners, scorers, catering facilities, visitor reception etc. Prizes should be prepared in advance and rosettes obtained in ample time.

Now the above is merely an outline reminder of what may be involved, but sufficient to indicate that a fair amount of work is involved in organising horse trials. Time is certainly required and if the planning is right then successful trials follow as a matter of course, always providing things are flexible enough to cope with any adverse changes in weather conditions. It is difficult to secure a site with perfect going over the whole area, but this must be borne in mind when planning in case it becomes very wet. Snow in April is a regular feature of some trials and a few arguably lucky ones can be baked hard in late summer which can be sore on horses too.

16

The Rider's View

It seems to have taken half a lifetime to get the horse schooled for the three-day event, or horse trials as we riders must learn to call them, with a perfectly ghastly winter trying to get in enough hunting to keep the enthusiasm and yet afraid to do too much in case a mishap knocks us out of the competition. Then with the turn of the year the frantic work to get up to top condition and yet careful not to reach peak too soon, with the almost constant care and attention, endless feeds, and mounting corn bills, one asks at that stage 'Really is it worth it?' knowing full well that there is no alternative. If you've built up preparations steadily over two years or more with just this end in view then there is certainly no backing down now.

The last few days are sensational. Everyone in the stables suddenly feels that this horse is going to do it, because he's bursting with fitness and keen to get out and go. So keen that it is desperately difficult trying to hold him back, and yet one dare not let rip or just possibly some pothole or a half bottle will be lying in wake and cut a foot or give a gash which will spell The End. It would be unbearable, especially after this final preparation when the horse gleams, the muscling is solid, and we think we have got positively everything we could need in a three months' let alone three days' period. The only thing left is for me to lose a few pounds, and, making the effort, I've hardly eaten a thing for days. The parents predict that as a result I shall be too weak to ride, and I'm frankly becoming suspicious that they could be right. . . .

We plan to get there early evening on the Tuesday, thankful that it is not a long journey for the box and giving Jack – his stable name – a pleasant work-out and going yet again through parts of that dratted dressage test. Seems to get no better, even if the girls say that it'll be fine on the day. That depends on whether he blows up on me or not, and in this state of fitness he is positively ready to explode. Restful afternoon and then the big pack-up. We're off and almost feeling complacent about it now.

At least we were until rounding the corner of one of those idyllic country lanes we suddenly saw a part of the cross-country course looming almost over the box height. My heart sank and stomach lurched at the thought of having to ride up to such an obstacle and clean over it. For two blades of straw I'd turn the box and go back home, except that the girls put on their challenging looks and I know that that's out of the question and so we must go through with it. Almost hope Jack will be found lame next morning. We get him unboxed and into the rather splendid loose box which has been allocated and suddenly he looks so good, munching up the evening feed, I've no doubt that he will be sound and ready for the test.

Next morning, Wednesday, we're all up before 6 am although goodness knows why with only one horse to do and so many volunteer helpers; besides it is not as if anything will happen today at all. We spend ages gossiping around, looking at the other horses, eyeing them up to see how they compare with ours and looking, hopefully, for any defects. The more that back out the better – there's no holds barred in this game. Then, as usual, that horrid outlook changes as we get to know the others; being replaced by a very good spirit really. We're all in it together suddenly and we don't want anyone backing out. We admit to being petrified together.

The ten o'clock briefing for competitors. This is it and in best military manner we are drawn into the campaign. Very matter-of-fact, a few flippances are permitted, but on the whole the approach is serious. First a reminder of any changes in the Rules, layout, or last-minute details. Then all eyes turned to the blackboard and course layouts and we start a quickfire run-through the main features and it is very fair and points to any potential trouble-spots. Outside it is bucketing down and we raise eyebrows at one another with a nod to the window. The Director, when finally unable to make himself heard through the din on the tin roof, breaks off and acknowledges that it is raining. With assurance he tells us that it is just a shower, and nothing to worry about as far as the going is concerned because it is near perfect and will soak that in nicely. We have our doubts – if he's been over-optimistic the reality will be a very soft surface and no grip.

After the briefing the questions. Newcomers such as I keep quiet, leaving the veterans to show their knowledge of the course and its changes. They even dare to argue with the Director at one point, but he manages to stay calm and adamant against making any changes. The talking is not prolonged and clearly everyone is anxious to be off round the course: we're driven over to save time and key features are explained on the spot. Obstacles never seem so big when in company with everyone trying not to show they are over-awed by anything. After lunch I walk the first part, trying to memorise it. That is when one realises that the fences have been put up a few feet higher since morning.

At teatime there is an examination of horses. We had Jack out for light exercise during the day, but he looks as if only a full gallop over the cross-country would settle him for any dressage on the morrow. Endless talking that night – all horses – then early to bed but over-excited and so check over the test yet again. Fall asleep panic-stricken that I have forgotten it altogether.

Very early start to Thursday to get some lunge-work done and then groom the horse as he's never been done before, plaiting up and all the frills. We're drawn early for dressage which will get it done with but would prefer more time to ride in and settle Jack, who is as jumpy as hell and seems likely to give me the reddest face on the ground. Big crowds already and looking at us so critically that I'm nearly as nervous as he is and still cannot remember the dressage test. Start riding in and suddenly we both forget the fuss going on around and settle to a really nice movement. Super to have such a fit horse and really responding. Reminds me that this is what horse trials are about really.

We're all looking superb in the sunshine, unbelievably smart after the last two days in casuals. Then it is us, trotting confidently to the front of the stand where a steward opens the ridiculously low white paling section to allow entry to the hallowed arena. Down the centre and a square halt. Hat off and force a smile to the jury of judges, who gravely nod back. So very correct and formal. Then off into the test, riding it mechanically and concentrating on Jack's every movement. Signals invisibly between us and it seems as if he knows and a gentle pressure from my legs sees response in his ears, and thankfully in pace too. It all seems too easy suddenly and too rashly I relax and we make a mistake and are past the marker before the transition. That will cost us for carelessness. Now it seems only seconds since we began until we're riding up that centre-line again to salute – have we forgotten a big chunk of the test perhaps? Forced smiles again, then out on a loose rein. Friendly steward opens those railings up to let us go and touches his bowler in a most respectful way. Perhaps it wasn't too bad after all, I dare to hope.

The marks for the test go up on the digital light boards but I cannot see them and wait impatiently for the news. It's all right for we're in the mid fifties and on present form that is about average. As the long day wears on there will be some about ten penalties less but lots much higher and so it is good and such a morale booster to start well instead of going into the endurance phase bogged down with handicap.

Walk the cross-country again – this time all the way round and pacing out the difficult obstacles and spreads, studying alternative ways to go and various approaches. Walk into the water and paddle around in bare feet to test the bottom. It's gravel but freezing cold and I dread the thought of being tipped in totally. There's a film show that evening for competitors and helpers, featuring horse trials, what else?

Next day (Friday) dressage tests continue, endlessly it seems. Depressing too as the scores seem to be improving and our good start is happening too often. Take Jack out for some serious work – just enough to clear the tubes and loosen up and not enough to tire or sweat up. He's fit and as ready for the big course as he'll ever be now although we would maybe have preferred to go a day earlier. Early to bed, dodging all the parties. Worn out with two more rounds of the course which I now know backwards and had the benefit of over-hearing spectators' views which seemed to be half in favour of it being bigger and the other half predicting it's a killer. Difficult to sleep on that one.

This is the great day (Saturday) and we're all up early and wishing we'd stayed in bed longer because of course nothing really happens until noon and even then some of them will not be on their way for ages. I'm drawn early and thankful for it. Everyone is nervous, jittery about the horses, and no-one is in the mood for talking about anything but the way the course is likely to ride after overnight rain.

We check the tack several times, feel Jack's legs repeatedly, and don't like to eat or drink much. But suddenly it is time to go and unbelievably we're not ready. Help! – a mad rush to tack up, watch safety points, strap on numbers and check watches. Remind helpers to be in the midway box with everything needed without fail and then it is to the Start – 3—2—1 and OFF.

Trotting off on the first roads and tracks with all the tensions suddenly flowing out of one, the tendency is to wonder what all the fuss was about. The horse is full of go, the day is glorious, and there is a great atmosphere without any of the pressure. A good steady pace and when we come to the long stretch on soft going I get Jack up into a bit of a gallop, just to see how he responds and as a check on how fast he can cover the ground if need be, and we drop back down quickly and finally almost canter up to the steeplechase start so as not to arrive before time. Ready? We've got exactly five minutes round this one. GO! A nicely paced gallop, keeping the horse pointed straight into the fences, flying along. Once round and check the watch – a shade fast, so easy there because we'll get no bonus points and we'll need every ounce of push for later. Crikey, we go into a slide at the last and for one awful moment I think we'll go through rather than over, but we lift off at the last minute and make it. Phew! That leaves me dripping and has shaken Jack somewhat as well so it's a bit of luck it was the last. Even so we've only just made the time with that hiccup. Now straight into the next phase of roads and tracks. Jack's looking just a bit blown so shall I jump off and walk or run alongside or just ease everything and let him walk until he's got his wind? Wasn't it Mary Gordon-Watson in the Olympics who was running alongside Cornishman and almost lost him. Panic stations! I decide to stay on top but decide I'd better put in some practice another time for this pacing caper – it could be necessary. Keep going – that much is essential and having gone over the route I think I know where to make up the time with speed.

Now we're wearing on and beginning to think of the ten minutes' compulsory break in the vet box, with great longing, I must say, and a few swigs of fruit juice will be most welcome. Seems to have been a long morning and of course it's now long past lunchtime with everything still in front of us. Mutter angrily and begin to feel that Jack hasn't got quite the push he had yesterday – well who the hell would have? Even if he is not pulling like a train any longer my arms feel as if they were taking it all and I keep looking at the watch to try and keep it all together to the last moment.

Into the box and the relief is unbearable. Everyone comes clamouring up with news, all speaking at once and I'm making nothing of it. Some get to work on the horse, others press a cup into my hand and I feel as if I'd like to have a lie down on the grass and shut my eyes away from everything. Items of news do penetrate through, like the ground being softish through the wood, and already two have come off at Fence 4. Cheering stuff I must say, and no-one mentions penalties so either it's bad and we've put up the blacks or else they don't know. Ten minutes just flies – the loo, a wash-down – back to the horse who's looking brisker again by some miracle and he's in the clear, so we're called and I'm up and off to the Start. Wheeling round, eager now and holding the brakes 3—2—1—GO! We're off over the first set of barrels without even knowing how we got there (either of us) but before the second the noise hits us. Whistles blow and the cry is carried along ahead of us 'Horse on course!' and taken up seemingly into infinity. I feel a bit like royalty with loudspeakers charting our way and the eager crowd of spectators willing us on either side of the track. Jack doesn't seem too bothered and has his nose stretched out and ears up ready for anything. Over the next little wall and the third will be easy too, but after that we've really got to think before we smash on. Think? Goodness I haven't a constructive thought in my head! Panics again and we're over three and suddenly I can mentally see the route just ahead, remembering that I want to turn in short to the fourth as otherwise there is a longer route and that will bring us in no straighter but seconds slower. Feels odd to be taking the initiative, but Jack seems to appreciate that he's got a rider in charge again and responds. We're over and I catch a murmur from the crowd as if we've done something odd (learn later that we were the first to turn in sharp to it). Big rails next out of the wood and dig the heels and ask – implore more likely – Jack to get up at it. We do, but rap it, which I suppose will teach him to pick up at these in future. He can't say that I didn't give warning that this was a big one. A set of in-and-out rails next which would have sent me into a dither but for the various walks round which finally persuaded me this one was all disguise. Just jump clean through the lot and don't give a fig for the alternatives. That was the trainers talking and they were right. That was the sixth – twenty-eight to go for goodness sake!

There's a nice lolloping ride along to the next one and we almost enjoy the interval, except that it also gives time to think about the big coffin and bank to come. Whistles shrilling, must be close, and the next turn brings it into sharp focus and also the first real doubts on tactics. What did they say about this one when we were in the box? Decide to do it as planned and jolly nearly come unstuck, because the ground is soft and someone's taken a slider and mucked it all up. I ask firmly, Jack hesitates – surely he won't refuse? – then pops in, a stride and over the ditch, and slithers fearfully but manages another pop out and we're through. Felt awful, really frightening and I didn't ride it at all. Lean over the horse's neck and clap it with real feeling. Gad, the horse is a marvel. And I recover and feel over-confident. Next there's one of these gimmicky dog kennel things and I decide to change now. Forget the script which opted for the easy way here, we'll go clean through and save some seconds. And we would have done, except that Jack runs out. For goodness sake, he refuses the stupid silly lump of horseflesh. I turn him round, furiously, pushing him on and defying him to do it again; nor does he this time and we fly the dashed things and leave them far behind in a oner. Nothing to the next heap of wood but I dig him just the same – no more nonsense and I'm riding now.

There's a bank ahead and a big crowd round obviously expecting plenty of sensations. Whistles and cries and a sea of faces but they can't know that this one's a doddle as horses merely have to be pushed up and a dig of the heels and they fly out the other side. Keep the balance I tell myself, as I suppose it is easy to get it wrong after all and perhaps go out the front or side door. But it is not a difficult obstacle, even if it may seem sensational. Big rails next and this could be dodgy as there's a lot of daylight beneath them, leaving no groundline. So I tell Jack and he listens, with the result that he's ready for it and even interested in this question. Leaves it with a clean flick of the heels and I can't resist looking back briefly to see as it's bigger on the far side. Anyhow we've a good going gallop to the water so here's the pressure off and a chance to make time.

For goodness sake the crowd around this pool seem to leave no room for horses. Suddenly I feel mad, thinking that they are all there just to see me go for a swim in that murky cold water. The thought, totally unreasonable, makes me determined to get through and I take a firm hold. There'll be no nonsense about this one – we're taking it slowly. They do say that it is the splashing and spray which makes horses duck out and I'm not risking that so we hop lazily in and paddle through only to find there's really not enough impulsion to get out so Jack almost banks it and struggles ... and struggles for a foothold. I'm helpless and the seconds tick, the crowd gasp and then cheer as he gets up and hops out. Phew! The relief of that one is incredible. Serves us right for ducking, giving the folks there a bit of a thrill – or did they get what they wanted? Sudden realisation that that one could count for three obstacles which means two more and we're half way.

Is that all? Seems as if we've been struggling for hours now. Suddenly realise that the horse is sweated up and not by any means as fresh as he was. Also that time is ticking out desperately. I ask for more and the old chap gives it, but not for very long and I have to ask again. Feel a bit of a heel about this. Over the pile of logs – not difficult because it can hardly be missed even by a tired horse and then come the gates and I've got Jack headed straight at them. Horrid feeling he's not going to lift and I duck ready for the crash, but in fact we're sailing over, even if the landing is a bit off balance. But then it takes seconds again to recover and get back in balance.

The next two or three flash by in a sort of daze, suppose I'm getting tired too. There's the big turf bank, the lane crossing which is up and down over the covered road surface and up and down again. He pecks again on landing which throws me off. Dashed nuisance this; becoming a habit and slows us down. Into the woods now, all light and shade and rather eerie. Think Jack's asleep and has not noticed anything different, give him a bit of stick coming out and up to the big sleeper table as sharp reminder we're still in business. It works and we're out. Then there are two sets of walls at an angle – big ones to be jumped cleanly so we get together again, dig with legs and sail up. Walls always look sickeningly tough but horses seem to respect them and get clear out of trouble, which is a relief because the falling would be merciless.

What have we got now? Dashed if I can remember where we are; almost as if I'd never walked the course. The feeder troughs loom up and I remember that this one is straight over without hesitation but the next is a massive zig-zag and I know which way to take that and ease down for it, ready for the short cut. Jack seems doubtful, heavens has he got another stop in him? A push and he takes off and it works as we've saved some seconds. I had planned to gallop on at top speed now to sail the next two without a care in the world, but suddenly I sense that the horse has very little left to give. He's all but out and there's nothing left when I squeeze, so instead it's to be a case of nursing on for the next few minutes. Getting what I can but keeping him going at all costs. I lean down and whisper, giving a clap on the neck which just about takes me out of the saddle and makes me realise I'm bushed as well. Horrible moment on the last but one – just a big log too – as I think we're going down. We rapped it hard and got off balance, but miraculously recovered and are still on our feet for the last obstacle. This is the sponsor's farewell and really just a shop counter. Does Jack know it is the last, if so how does he know? I haven't time to puzzle it out but I think he does know and goes at it like the clappers and we gallop on up the straight as if jet-propelled and I even begin to wonder how I'll stop him going into the crowd. Loose rein, total exhaustion, but the most wonderful feeling of achievement – we got round. I almost yell it out and feel silly. The gang haul us in and it is saddle off and into the weigh-in tent. Must have lost pounds, but in fact have not. We got round!

The triumph is rather short-lived. Especially when I am told the hard truth that we not only had a refusal but there will be time penalties because we took our time and gave no-one the impression of hurrying, even if we did think we'd taken some short cuts. Other riders are making the time, even if there is a trail of havoc too. Totally spent, the temporary elation of having got round at all is soon past, especially when I see Jack looking so totally knackered. It really isn't fair, or worth it. Still we can always say we got round. . . .

Back to the stables, a brush down, light feed and rest. I clean-up, drink a coffee and can't rest, even if it is totally masochistic to watch one's colleagues all over the course again. Wonder how on earth others do manage to ride more than one in the day over such a course. Still there is satisfaction there – it has proved something. Besides we might not finish bottom of the starters.

Much later that night there is a dance in the village hall. How could we hope to do even a circuit of the floor? Surprisingly everyone does dress up and go, and mighty relaxed we are too. The thrills are over and we've got round – or at least some of us have. There are absentees of course. Back at the stables they say some will be working all night to try and get their charges past the veterinary surgeons in the morning parade. Our party leaves the dance early, just to go back to stables and check. There's a bit of heat in the legs, but we've been told that this is not abnormal at this stage. Renew the bandages, soothe them down and leave Jack to rest, which is what he wants to do above everything else – even eating – although he's had enough to convince us that there's nothing far wrong.

Up early next morning. Everyone is working furiously to get horses fit enough, beat the stiffness and make 'em walk out. At ten there's the parade and a lot of them look distinctly groggy too. As time goes on, however, they seem to loosen up and walk out well enough to pass. Any doubtfuls seem to have been taken out overnight, which seems a sensible thing to do.

There's a church service after the parade, but we don't all go. After lunch everyone is dolled up in show-jumping habit and the horses transformed too, and even eager again bless them. That includes Jack, who takes part in the parade of all competitors with a good bit of his old bounce back. Then into the final phase over a reasonable set of jumps. They seem small and some of the horses appear to know that these are not solid obstacles but that if they rap them the poles will go. Accordingly, some almost appear to make a point of it, which must be totally infuriating to riders previously in with a chance.

Positions are changing a bit now and being early in the draw we get out there and go almost round before Jack kicks back and has one down. Hard to keep a smile on one's face when that happens. Still we were not expecting a place and so the pressure is not as severe as for those with everything still to jump for and for whom the slightest mistake means demotion. As it happens the leaders in this one do not waver but farther down the line they change quite a lot. In the end we finish half-way up, and for a first crack at the big trials everyone seems to think that that is a pretty good result from which we can go on strongly. My own reaction is relief that Jack is through the lesson without a mark. We box up for home and on arrival he snickers with pleasure at being back in his own box. Soon he'll be turned out and roughed off, until early summer when we'll start all over again, getting fit for the next big one. Only this time we'll both be more experienced and be going all out for a place.

17

The Future

It has been calculated that if horse trials as a sport continue to develop at the present rate there could be over 20,000 horses engaged in 120 trials in a season in Britain alone, within a very short time. World-wide the impact would be significant and there is not the slightest reason to suppose that this will not be the case as efforts are made to engage our attentions more and more in sport of all kinds and to give people the leisure time to enjoy them, whether participating actively or as spectators.

Nevertheless there are many question marks centred on the future pattern of horse trials, not least in the cost of competing at the higher levels and the effect of bigger and more testing courses on valuable animals. Plus the fact that as a result of expansion there must be more demand for facilities, both for training and for holding trials. It does require wide open spaces for a good galloping ground and these may not be easily come by in the future. The training will be easier, because we believe in it and want to give our young riders every possible opportunity and facility. Hopefully, though, more local authorities and sports organisers will extend their bounties to equestrian sports which are too often dismissed as being the preserves of the mythical rich requiring no assistance.

The major area of concern nowadays is not that the support will not be there at what is tiresomely called 'the grass-roots' but that the pyramid formed by eager Pony Club and other supporters will not peak with the elite riders which have, and continue to, reflect such honour on their countries and draw international acclaim for their exploits and skills.

It is sometimes suggested that it may become impossibly difficult to campaign with well-mounted and equipped teams, able to tackle the very big courses now commonplace internationally. This is nonsense and I can see little indication of this ever being the case, so long as countries have keen competition for their squad places and providing sense prevails in the task set for the horsemen. It is still an honour to be selected to ride for one's country and this has to be the ultimate ambition of everyone engaged in competition. We must do nothing to devalue the prestige or to under-estimate the degree of skills and competence required to be in with a chance of glorious achievement.

Should courses continue to get bigger year by year? Obviously not, because there are limits to endurance and occasional signs that they are being reached if not going a bit over the top. For all this I do believe that the ingenuity of course builders can manage to pose questions and add spectator appeal to obstacles without over-taxing our horses. The trick is not so much in dimensions of height and breadth as in solving the riddle of the best means of approach, of judging the strides, and in co-ordinating the effort between horse and rider. Suggestions have been made that the roads and tracks phase serves no purpose and could be eliminated without loss to the three-day trials, and after all they are excluded from lesser events. It is, however, generally agreed that this would be a mistake and that the general wind-up to the cross-country as at present is a good thing and distance is a feature of endurance. Moreover it is felt that with adequate roadwork preparation no particular problems should be presented. It is always easy to propose reducing the trials, but problematical as to what might be substituted in place, and on balance it is agreed that the formula of the overall test is about right. There is, too, the other argument, which is ongoing, about the place of the show-jumping phase in the whole trial. If it is too stiff a course it is felt to be unfair and conversely if not catching any combinations out then it is held to be not severe enough. There are certainly occasions when this phase has been too simple a test and it is desirable that it be set so as to exert sufficient influence and provide some sort of a spectator interest as well. It is all a matter of balance between the different phases and care must be taken to ensure that none outweighs the other in importance and has undue influence on the level of penalty points incurred. Nor do I think we should organise trials in such a way that they are purely directed to staging a spectator sport – there is happy medium between catering to all requirements and remembering that above all else the objective is that of testing horse and rider. All else comes second to that one.

Surprisingly enough, running horse trials can be quite profitable, even though the impression is given that they must be heavily subsidised. One wonders sometimes if organisers are being perfectly fair to competitors, in that their costs are extremely high and they take all the risk with the odds distinctly against hopes of financial reward. Hopefully we shall see some improvement here, because owners must get recompense if they are to campaign horses. Sponsorship has given the sport the injection of support and cash which it needed and the results speak for themselves, but it does remain a hobby for those with the means and there must be many promising youngsters unable to get far as a result of event horses being priced out of reach. There is a scope in this direction for sponsors and we shall surely see this aspect develop in much the same way as has show-jumping but hopefully without some of the abuses which crept in and resulted in horses changing names so frequently that the public simply could not follow their favourites at all.

Horse management is a subject of special interest to many of us and in this respect I think we still have much to learn and relate to horse trials. Already increasing interest in long-distance riding is contributing to knowledge, so far as endurance is concerned, and the more we know about the way a horse responds and how much is taken out of it by severe conditions, the better we can prepare it and get it through the test. The current American interest in what is known as 'interval training' is of special interest in that it presents a new approach to preparation. The tendency to keep a trials horse working perpetually up to a peak of condition for the day imposes rather unnecessary strains all round and psychologically a reduced pressure may well show better results. We are apt to treat horses as athletes, without at the same time giving them the benefit of the human athlete's freedom of choice. They can be brought to condition, trained to a high pitch, and made obedient to a particular rider, but all that may not be sufficient if the mood of the moment is wrong and it cannot be forced.

One of the fascinations for riders as competitors is that no two horses are the same and so their approaches have to change with each. It means that the horse trials scene is constantly changing as new combinations are put together and work-out. Sometimes, too, the results are quite disastrous, and one wonders why trainers persist when a change of jockey could make much better use of the mount. Spectators in this respect can often see more of the game than those actually involved in it!

Should there be teams in horse trials? This is an intriguing question and one which is likely to be asked more frequently in the future. This is because riding in trials is an individual thing and a matter of horse and rider in combination working things out together. With teams the accent is purely on winning, with the additional restraint of responsibility to the other members which tends to determine the course of action. This is not in the spirit of trials at all when you come to think of it, so there can be little justification for team engagement, nor any value excepting illusory international honour. An individual winning effort will always be more meritorious than a team effort, simply because the latter depends on a good average and getting home regardless of the strain on rider or horse. Many a time experience has shown that tactics for a team place are entirely out of keeping with those for a sensible individual effort. Equally there have been countless incidences of an injured rider continuing simply in order that the team should not be let down; even worse are cases in which a horse has been pushed beyond endurance for the same reasons. This is inexcusable and a quite pointless exercise which should not be encouraged. The emphasis should be placed on individual performance, which is the essence of the trial, and, no matter the final place, it will have been the best that horse and rider could in the circumstances attain, and also a fair and reasonable indication of their ranking.

It is important for the future of horse trials that we get the priorities right and hold to them, thus providing a set of standards by which to judge performance. It is a competitive sport, but the winning should be secondary to the taking part or participation and the achievement of a reasonable placing and a fair trial.

We tend to emphasise the horse and its performance, but I am not so sure that the riding should not be given more weight. Horse trials have the great virtue of requiring skill all-round and to achieve any sort of a result competitors must train and must condition their horses and themselves. It would be fair to say that the growth of this sport has done more than anything else to improve the overall standard of riding at all levels. Even as spectators watching trials on the ground or on the television we do become aware of the very great feats of riding which we see in competition. We begin to appreciate the subtleties of dressage and the way in which horses are made obedient in response to good riding. The result is that every time we hack out, something of these examples linger with us, and still more so if we are aiming higher in competition.

There must be increasing emphasis in the future on the standard of riding and we can confidently expect it to go higher and higher, to the very great benefit of all equestrian sport and interests. Good riding and close sympathy with the horse are synonymous with any sort of success in horse trials and this cannot and should not be forgotten. Sometimes one sees a rider flinging about in the saddle over show-jumps and getting away with it, but the same sort of approach in horse trials would be useless. Even if it worked on one phase it would result in failure in another, thank goodness, because there is no place for the casual undisciplined approach, and it can never yield long-term results.

So we leave horse trials confident that they have a future role in equestrian sports, and certain that there will be continuing expansion. The more the public become involved and knowledge-able about the disciplines, the greater will the support and under-standing be. The objectives are simple, the achieving of them tough and demanding, but the tangible reward is total satisfaction and grand sport.

Glossary

Refer also to index

Action   The way the horse moves its legs.
Aids   Signals of rider to horse.

Blown   A winded horse, puffed.
Box   Area for veterinary inspection.
Break   To alter stride or break to harness, train.

Cadence   Rhythm of movement or pace.
Cavaletti   A small jump.
Change of rein   Going from left to right or vice versa.
Classical airs   High school riding, advanced dressage.
Coffin   Type of obstacle.
Collection   Riding horse up to bit, so that head is lowered and hocks engaged.
Combined training   Earlier phase for horse trials.
Concours complet   French term for trials.
Course   Cross-country route.
Cough, the   Form of equine 'flu.

Diagonals   Horse's opposite hind and fore leg movement.
Discipline   The particular or specialised branch of equine sport.
Doping   Use of illegal substances.
Dressage   French to prepare, to train.

Endurance   Part of cross-country phase.
Event   Horse trial.
Extension   Extended stride of horse, stepping right out.

Fault   Penalty or points loss.
FEI   *Federation Equestre Internationale* – international organising body.

Girth   Circumference of belly, strap over the same.
Grading   System by points awarded on placings.
Groundline   Base of jump giving clear sight of obstacle.
Green horse   Untrained or raw Novice.

Hack   Informal leisure ride.
Half-halt   Check on rein to signal transition of pace.
Half-pass   Horse moving forequarters on different line to hind.
Heat   In leg-swelling.
Hors concours   Not part of team, riding as individual competitor.

Impulsion   Forward movement, speed.
Interval training   System of training allowing break in discipline.

Jockey Club   Ruling body for racing.
Jury   Judges.

Laterals   Fore and hind legs moving on same side.
Lunge   Long schooling rein.

Manège   Schooling arena.
Markers   Dressage arena signs.
Martingale   Part of tack to control head.
Medium trot   Medium pace, not too fast.
Mother pace   Term used for the walk.

Needle   Injection syringe.

Obstacles   Cross-country jumps.
Oxer   Type of obstacle.
Overface   Over tested at obstacle.

Penalties   System of marking.
Phase   Different stage or section of trials.
Piaffe   Dressage movement performed on one spot, i.e. without forward movement.

Pocket   Another word for 'box' for veterinary inspection.
Put down   To destroy, slaughter.

Rapping   Illegal means of training by raising jump pole as horse
  goes over.
Rat-catcher   Phrase for informal dress, tweed jackets.
Rein-back   Steps backwards.
Renvers   Half pass on two tracks.
Rules   As laid down by governing body for sport.
Run-in   Last part of cross-country to finish.
Run-out   Avoidance of obstacle.

Set fair   Leave tidy.
Shoulder-in   Forehand on different track to hind quarters.
Skewbald   Colour of horse – brown/white patches.
Snaffle   Type of bit.
Spin   Eliminate on veterinary grounds.
Squad   Team.
Steeplechase   As in racing, an endurance phase.
Stop   A refusal.
Stride   A distance.
Spooking   Nervous reaction, startled.

Tack   Saddlery.
Tact   Ride with understanding.
Test   Dressage test.
Track   Course or path.
Transitions   Alterations in pace.
Trakehner   Type of obstacle, also breed of horse.
Tracking-up   Hind foot following into steps of fore.
Travers   Half pass, two-tracks.

Warming-up   To ride in, loosen up.

Index